Programs for Asian Global Legal Professions Series Ⅴ

Promoting the Rule of Law
in Asian Dynamics

Edited by
KEIGLAD

KEIGLAD
Keio Institute for Global Law and Development

The publication was produced by KEIGLAD
KEIGLAD - Keio Institute for Global Law and Development
Keio University, 2-15-45 Mita, Minato-ku, Tokyo 108-8345 Japan
http://keiglad.keio.ac.jp/en/

Distributed by KEIO UNIVERSITY PRESS INC.
2-19-30 Mita, Minato-ku, Tokyo 108-8346 Japan
http://www.keio-up.co.jp/kup/eng/

ISBN 978-4-7664-2728-8
Printed in Japan

PREFACE

Legal education is experiencing rapid globalization. To meet the demand, Keio University Law School aims to develop law programs at universities throughout Asia. In 2015, our faculty and partner universities in the Mekong region countries launched, "Programs for Asian Global Legal Professions (PAGLEP)," a joint program fostering legal professions to solve legal issues from global perspectives.

Keio University Law School has established legal education research projects in Japan and the Mekong region countries in the teaching methods of private and public law. For law students, we promoted bilateral and multilateral law programs in Hanoi, Ho Chi Minh City, Phnom Penh, Vientiane, Bangkok, Yangon, and Tokyo.

Thanks to the support from our partner universities and collaboration from all the program participants, our results have been published in "Programs for Asian Global Legal Professions (PAGLEP) Series," Volume One to Four.

2020 was a milestone year for the PAGLEP. Unfortunately, the impact of the COVID-19 pandemic forced universities to postpone all in-person international programs. Despite this crisis, our universities worked diligently to develop online programs in law and international collaboration. I am convinced the outcome will be fruitful.

This book, Volume Five of the PAGLEP Series, is a part of them. It includes presentations and discussions at the PAGLEP Symposium 2020: University's Contribution toward "the Rule of law Ubiquitous World" held on 21 November, 2020, by way of the Internet. Online legal education will cultivate a new paradigm of research, development, collaboration, and connection among professors and students in Asia.

The new path will grant access to anyone interested in legal education whenever and wherever they are. We hope it will be a democratizing tool for the rule of law promotion in Asia, which is the central theme of this volume.

Finally, I convey sincere gratitude to the Ministry of Education, Culture, Sports, Science, and Technology in Japan for their continuous support. Due to their financial contribution over the last five years, we met our goal of opening a new dimension of research on collaborated legal education and the rule of law promotion in Asia.

Isao Kitai

Professor and Dean, Keio University Law School

10 January 2021

OPENING REMARK

at the Symposium on University's Contribution
toward "the Rule of Law Ubiquitous World"

The Programs for Asian Global Legal Professions (PAGLEP) Symposium 2020 is being held in unprecedented circumstances this year during the COVID-19 pandemic. We would like to express our great appreciation to Keio University as the organizing school for their efforts to hold this symposium.

The Inter-University Exchange Project, for which Keio University was one of the universities selected, aims to strengthen the global network of Japanese universities by offering high-quality education that is compatible with international programs. Our objective to promote strategic student exchanges and collaborative programs that have met quality assurance standards with universities in countries and regions that are important to Japan.

Under this initiative, to date, a total of 32 new projects targeting the ASEAN countries have been selected over four periods: three in fiscal 2011, fourteen in 2012, seven in 2013, and eight in 2016.

At the end of the subsidy period, Keio University Law School has continued to carry out various initiatives, such as the establishment of the Foundation for Legal Education in Asia, in order to maintain a steady stream of international students from the Mekong countries and other countries in Asia.

With the big boost given by the Inter-University Exchange Project, the number of Japanese and international students who have participated in exchanges with the ASEAN nations has dramatically increased, from 3,416 Japanese outbound students in 2011 to 21,865 in 2018, and from 13,400 inbound international students in 2011 to 96,736 in

2019.

This fiscal year, the COVID pandemic has seriously impacted the internationalization of university education by sharply restricting student and faculty mobility. Nevertheless, through ingenuity and cooperation, and by taking advantage of advantages like small time differences, within the consortium of universities, we have seen a number of international education and exchange programs conducted online, including the joint webinar held by students of the collaborating universities in September of this year. For now, we would like universities to maintain their collaborations and continue to advance their efforts for high-quality student exchanges even during the pandemic.

Lastly, we sincerely hope this symposium will prove of great value for the further development of projects between Keio and the other collaborating universities.

Representative, the Office for International Planning, Higher Education Bureau, the Ministry of Education, Culture, Sports, Science, and Technology (MEXT)
21 November 2020

CONTENTS

PART I

Chapter 1

THE RULE OF LAW PROMOTION IN ASIAN DYNAMICS:

Toward the Rule of Law Ubiquitous World

Hiroshi Matsuo*

(Keio Universiy)

1. Introduction: Issues on the Rule of Law Promotion in the Asian Context

Since the 1960s, countries in East and Southeast Asia have achieved rapid and sustained economic growth. Among its possible reasons, some economists and political scientists focused on the role of political regimes described as "the developmental state," in which technocratic bureaucrats devised and implemented rational plans based on development policies.[1] Those bureaucrats were protected by government leaders, which tended to be "authoritarian,"[2] though they maintained cooperative relationships with the private sector.[3]

---

* Professor, Keio University Law School, and Director, Keio Institute for Global Law and Development.

[1] As for the meaning of the developmental state, see Johnson 1982: pp. 17-33.

[2] For instance, on the authoritarian nature of the Japanese government, see Johnson 1982: pp. 37, 270. However, there are different types of authoritarian regime and Japanese one is different from Korean one (ibid., pp. 316-317). For the Authoritarian regimes in Southeast Asia, see Morgenbesser 2020.

[3] World Bank 1993: p. 13. Besides, for some democratic elements in the authoritarian government, see Studwell 2013: p. xxvi.

However, state-led rapid growth managed by government officials has had some side effects. The democratic control of political powers exercised by governments with authoritarian tendencies has been central problems related to the process of economic development, such as structured corruption ("kōzō-oshoku" in Japanese) caused by the coalition of bureaucrats, politicians, and businesses.[4] The authoritarian nature of government is not the same, even within East and Southeast Asian countries,[5] and the problems experienced by individual states vary. But issues on the control of government powers have repeatedly mattered in each of these countries' development context.

In a recent case in Japan, the Cabinet decided on 31 January 2019 that the retirement age of 63 years for public prosecutors[6] shall be extended for an additional six months, particularly for Mr. K. It was an extraordinary Cabinet decision without any legal ground. For ordinary government officials, there is a provision for the extension of the retirement age under certain circumstances, for example, due to the special expertise of a particular official who cannot be replaced by another official for the moment.[7] It aims to avoid serious harm to the public interest. But this provision shall not be applied to public prosecutors because the Law on Public Prosecutors is enacted as a special law to the Law on Central Government Officials, and there is no provision on the extension of the retirement age in the Law on Public Prosecutors to avoid political intervention in the prosecutor's personnel. The government has officially confirmed this interpretation[8], and it had been kept in practice without exception until the Cabinet decision on 31 January 2019, as mentioned above. In response to the critics, the Prime Minister responded on 13 February 2020 that the Cabinet had changed the former interpretation of the relevant provision of the Law on Central Government Officials to the effect that it shall be applied to public prosecutors. Subsequently, on 16 April

---

[4] For the governmental corruption scandals in Japan, see Johnson 1982: p. 68 with note 83.

[5] Johnson 1982: pp. 316-317.

[6] Section 22 of the Law on Public Prosecutors Office.

[7] Section 81-3 of the Law on Central Government Officials.

[8] For instance, the remark by the Director of General Office, Personnel Bureau on 28 April 1981.

2020, the Cabinet submitted a Bill to Amend the Law on Public Prosecutors that enabled the Cabinet to decide on the extension of the retirement age for certain high-ranked prosecutors within one year after turning 63 years old. Further criticism was levied by former prosecutors, including the former Prosecutor General to the Minister of Justice, on 15 May 2020.[9] This incident illustrates the current state of the rule of law in Japan through the treatment of a provision of a particular law by the government, which is thought to be authoritarian.[10]

Recently, government measures for the COVID-19 pandemic have also been important issues concerned with the rule of law. What are the correct restrictions on people's free activities to protect their lives and health from infectious disease in the name of the public interest? In Japan, the Special Measures Law for Countermeasures against the New Influenza, etc. (SMLCNI)[11] was amended in response to the COVID-19 pandemic. On 26 March 2020, the Headquarters for the Control of New Coronavirus Infectious Disease was established within the Cabinet Secretariat based on Sec. 15 (1) SMLCNI. However, measures to avoid the spreading of the epidemic taken by the SMLCNI are currently very limited,[12] and the government cannot take any compulsory measures to restrict people's activities. It is difficult to coordinate effective measures from the viewpoint of security as a whole and the freedom of individuals. What is the most effective legal response to the COVID-19 pandemic? Which country has been the most

---

[9] The Opinion of the Volunteers of Former Prosecutor, drafted by Isao Shimizu, 15 May 2020, *Asahi Shimbun*, 16 May 2020, p. 29.

[10] The Opinion (Fn. 9) criticized the change of interpretation of Sec. 81-3 of the Law on Central Government Officials (see Fn. 7 and the corresponding text) announced by the Prime Minister on 13 February 2020 as it is reminiscent of Louis XIV (1638-1715) who said "I am the State." See also Fn. 2 supra.

[11] Law No. 31, 2012.

[12] In the state of emergency announced by the central government (Sec. 32 SMLCNI), (i) the prefectual governor may request the inhabitants necessary cooperation and the manager of certain facilities measures necessary to avoid infections; (ii) if the manager of facilities did not follow the request without justifiable reason, the prefectural governor may instruct the manager necessary measures; and (iii) the prefectual governor must publicly announce that the request and instruction were given to the manager of facilities (Sec. 45 SMLCNI).

successful in managing it? The difference in the number of infected persons and the mortality rate from country to country divides the evaluation of restrictive governments' measures between reevaluating the authoritarian system on the one hand and warning against surveillance and controlled society on the other.[13]

Furthermore, democracy promotion and human rights protections are major objectives to which the rule of law is expected to contribute through the management of government powers. Access to legal information that the government holds, compensation for damages caused by government actions, the protection of the rights of minorities, children, workers, etc., have all tended to be subordinated to the developmental issues prioritized by authoritarian governments in the developmental state.[14]

But, issues on the rule of law are not limited to the control of the political powers of authoritarian governments, as discussed above. The rule of law presupposes that the law can bind people backed by the centralization of government powers. There are two sides to the promotion of the rule of law, in the sense that the law can on the one hand bind people, and on the other hand bind the government. However, it is not easy to achieve both at the same time. There is a dilemma in that the former must be a prerequisite for the latter[15], and countries in East and Southeast Asia are still seeking to strengthen the binding force of law, yet strengthened powers are difficult to restrain.

There is no fixed answer to this puzzle. However, our experiences in Asian countries can provide some suggestions for possible solutions, although they will vary depending on each country's political and economic conditions. Even within the countries of East and Southeast Asia, the people and governments are facing different problems of the rule of law, suggesting that the concept, structure, and method of promotion of the rule of law may be flexible per a country's development process.

---

[13] For the rule of law approach to issue on the COVID-19 pandemic, see 2.2 infra.

[14] These issues are treated in the following chapters in this Part.

[15] That the law must be capable of being obeyed is the original sense of law and the basic idea of the rule of law. See Raz 2009: pp. 212-214.

2. The Use of Law as a Government's Measure to Promote Economic Development

2.1 The Rule *of* Law versus Rule *by* Law?

It is recognized that governments played a central role in achieving the remarkable economic growth from the 1960s to the 1980s in Korea, Taiwan, Hong Kong, Singapore, Malaysia, Indonesia, Thailand, and Japan, called the High Performing Asian Economies (HPAEs). They did so by implementing various economic policies[16], including industrial policy, financial policy, export promotion policy, medium- and long-term planning policy, and infrastructure provision policy, such as a railway, port, airport, communication facilities, electric power, etc. For instance, governments selectively intervened in industries, and they gave them financial supports and tax privileges to enhance their competitive strength, which was linked with the stimulation of exports and contributed to swift economic growth in Korea, Taiwan, Malaysia, Singapore, and Japan[17]. The governments passed special laws to implement those policies.

The legislation seemed to have three meanings. Firstly, it was used as an anchor to prevent political interference by opposition parties, making the policies difficult to be changed, and facilitating their precise execution. Secondly, the legislation of policies secured a source of financing from the government budget. And thirdly, it was regarded as a type of social contract which helped governments gain the understanding of the citizens for the legislated policy and contributed to providing a platform for cooperation between the state and the private sector[18]. The instrumental usage of the law can also be seen in China, Vietnam, and Laos since the middle of the 1980s when they introduced market mechanisms.

However, when authoritarian governments use legislation as a nominal jus-

---

[16] World Bank 1993: pp. 1-3.

[17] Matsuo 2016: Chapter 6, Section 2; Chapter 7, Section 2; Chapter 8, Section 1, 2, Chapter 9, Section 2; Chapter 10, Section 2.

[18] Matsuo 2016: the last paragraph of Section 2, Chapter 6.

tification of development policies without deliberated discussion in the assembly and by restraining the opposition both inside and outside the assembly, it can cause critical reactions from civil society alleging that their substantial rights have been affected. Such an instrumental usage of the law by authoritarian governments has been often criticized as "rule by law" as opposed to the rule of law.[19] But is it always correct to conceptualize rule by law as the opposite of the rule of law? Various aspects have been developed around the concept of rule by law and its relationship with the rule of law.[20] It depends on the conception of

---

[19] For instance, the term of "rule by law" is used to mean "the use of the legal form as a cloak for arbitrary power", or "the use of law as a tool of abuse." See Balasubramaiam 2008: p. 211. However, it recognizes two other "non-prejorative" ways of understanding rule by law: (i) an avoidable side-effect of legal order that the law is not always successful in discipling political power even when the legislator conscientiously attempted to impose such discipline; (ii) the idea which is more akin to the rule of law understood as a moral idea (ibid., pp. 211-212, note 3). On the rule of law and rule by law in Singapore, see Silverstein 2008: p. 1131; Rajah 2012.

[20] They include Lugosi 2003, Silverstein 2008, Balasubramaniam 2008, Rajah 2012, Tushnet 2014, Li 2015, Ng 2019, Waldron 2019.

A comprehensive review of the contrasts between rule by law and the rule of law is given by Waldron 2019. (i) The most common contrast is: under rule by law, law is used by the authoritarian government as an instrument to achieve the political ends, but it is not used to control the government itself (legal authoritarianism); under the rule of law, the government itself is constrained by law (government subjection to law) (ibid., pp. 3-6). (ii) Another contrast between them is found in the different conception of law: under the rule by law, the law is understood as enacted legislation and government regulation; under the rule of law, the law includes that is not subject to government, that is, "autonomous law" such as common law and customary law (or natural law) (ibid., pp. 12-13). The legal thought might have influenced the distinction (ibid., pp. 10-12). The supporters of neo-liberal thought dislike the legislative and regulatory restrictions on free transactions to be imposed by the discretionary government.

The term "rule by law" has often been used in a critical context as the antithesis of the rule of law. In this context, rule by law is a "debased version of the rule of law," and rule "by" law adopts "a much maligned" usage of a preposition (ibid., p. 3). However, it is questioned whether the difference between rule by law and the rule of law is a difference of kind or a difference of degree. Rule by law can be distinguished from rule by the despotic government that does not use law at all (rule by law can be the antithesis of rule by evil men). The legality, which rule by law implies, can be interpreted as demanding the rule of law. And the rule of law cannot restrain all government actions for the public good. If these points are consid-

rule by law and the rule of law. The contrast between rule by law and the rule by law is correlated with the contrast between formal definition and substantive definition of the rule of law.

According to the formal definition of the rule of law, it is recognized as existing when a state has a set of articulated laws made by a legislature, the laws are precisely executed by a reliable executive, and a conflict can be solved by a judgment which is given in an open court of an independent judiciary in an open trial and is equally enforced.[21] The formal conception of the rule of law can be compatible with rule by law as it means the use of political power through law.[22] The government can effectively regulate people's actions through legislation. However, it cannot guarantee that the content of the law is "good" enough such that it substantially protects the people's rights. In this sense, the formal definition can be considered a "thin" definition[23] or "rule-book" conception of the rule of law[24].

---

ered, the difference between rule by law and the rule of law is subtle and not the difference of kind, and the usefulness of the distinction is beginning to evaporate (ibid., pp. 14-21).

I agree with Waldron's review of rule by law that it captures "a considerable element of what the rule of law is supposed to involve" (ibid., p. 23). The problem is how we should identify the elements that make up the entire structure of the rule of law. As a tentative assumption, I will capture figuratively the entire structure of the rule of law as a three-story building, in which the first and second stories correspond to the elements of rule by law. See the text corresponding to note 39 in 3.3 infra.

[21] For the summary of formal definition, see Stephenson 2001; Matsuo 2005: p. 59. J. Raz who defends the formal conception developed it in 8 principles. See Raz 2009: pp. 214-219.

[22] We should not regard the rule of law defined in a formal sense as the same as rule by law, because there are variations in the formal rule of law and in rule by law so that they do not always overlap each other. However, if we understand the concept of rule by law not in the negative sense but in the positive sense that even the authoritarian government shall exercise its political power through law, which is stipulated in advance by a legislature, executed precisely by officials, and adjudicated in a particular case by the independent court, rule by law shares largely common elements with the rule of law in the formal definition.

[23] Peerenboom 2004: p. 2. A thin conception focuses on the formal or instrumental aspects of rule of law.

[24] Dworkin 1985: p. 11. The rule-book conception insists that the state's power should never

If we follow the substantive definition and identify the rule of law with the rule of good law, rule by law must be distinguished from the rule of law because government actions to be characterized as rule by law may infringe on the rights of the people, which should be provided according to the good law that is normatively just and right.[25] According to this conception, the rule of law is not necessarily sufficient, even with the existence of laws enacted by the legislature, executed precisely by the executive, and interpreted by the independent judiciary; it is only so if the substantial content of the law is recognized as normatively just and right. In this sense, the substantive definition is considered the "thick" definition[26] or the "rights" conception of the rule of law[27]. Under the substantive understanding of the rule of law, the government should primarily protect the life of the people, guarantee freedom of the people's actions, and manage the balance between regulation and freedom.

Why is the definition of the rule of law split into two (or more) meanings?[28] The reason is that we can be satisfied neither with the formal definition nor with the substantive definition. Two (or more) definitions would converge if we had a completed legal system which is equipped with good laws with perfect integrity, rightly created and enforced by a strong government, and voluntarily obeyed by

---

be exercised against individual citizens except in accordance with rules explicitly set out in a public rule book available to all. It implies that not only the government but also ordinary citizens must play by these public rules until they are changed, in accordance with further rules about how they are to be changed, which are also set out in the rule book.

[25] For the summary of substantive definition, see Stephenson 2001; Matsuo 2005: p. 59.

[26] Peernboom 2004: p. 4. A thick (or substantive) conception incorporates elements, in addition to the basic elements of the thin conception, of political morality such as economic arrangements, government forms, or human rights conceptions.

[27] Dworkin 1985: pp. 11-12. The rights conception assumes that citizens have moral rights and duties one another, and political rights against the state as a whole. These moral and political rights shall be recognized in positive law and enforced.

[28] On the functional definition of the rule of law, which focuses on "how well the law and legal system perform some function" such as constraining the government discretion, making legal doctrines predictable, etc., see Stephenson 2001. It seems to include both elements of the formal and substantive definition.

the people; a perfect state with good laws, good government and good govern-ance will find the right answer in response to any questions. But where is such a legal system? Nowhere. Then, if we followed the formal definition, it would be dangerous to blindly follow the law legislated by the authority of the govern-ment. As our experiences tell us, the legislated law might infringe on the basic rights of the people. But if we follow the substantive definition, it may be diffi-cult to identify which law is good, just, and right objectively, and we would not be able to determine what the law is when different views are competing on the goodness, justness, and rightness of the content of the law. This is the dilemma that is inherent to the definition of the rule of law.

However, this dilemma seems to be caused by the very question which asks abstractly and statically, "*what is* the rule of law?" It seems to be a classroom question rather than an empirical and practical question. In reality, especially in the development process of a country, the question of what the rule of law is can hardly be separated from the question of *how* the rule of law *is created, devel-oped and established.* If we combine the question of what the rule of law is with the question of how it is established in the development process of a country, the formal definition of the rule of law can be compromised with the substan-tive definition by dividing development into stages: the early stage, in which the rule of law by the formal definition shall be installed, and the advanced stage, in which the rule of law by the substantive definition should be implemented.[29]

From the viewpoint of this dynamic conception of the rule of law as a pro-cess starting from the formal and the thin rule of law and developing toward the substantive and the thick rule of law, the element of rule by law can be included

---

[29] This sequential conception of the rule of law starting from the formal or thin to the substantive or thick rule of law would not contradict with the recognition that "the core meaning" or "basic element" of the rule of law refers to a system in which law can impose restraints on the government, because the latter recognition of the rule of law is described in contast to "a rule by law." See Peerenboom 2004: p. 2. Similarly, Tamanaha recognizes as "the first cluster" of the rule of law meaning that the government is limited by the law, in contrast to "the second cluster" which is characterized as the "formal legality" or "the rule by rules." Tamanaha 2004: pp. 137-141.

in the process of establishing the rule of law to be coordinated by the concept of good governance of a state. The reason is that in the development process, the rule of law is not an independent goal but is rather an instrument for achieving the more comprehensive goal of good governance of the state.[30]

As mentioned above, during the development process of the countries of East and Southeast Asia, which experienced rapid and sustained economic growth under government leadership, governments must have been strong enough to devise and implement development plans by the instrumental use of the law. In this process, "rule by law" has been in the construction process of the rule of law as a part of good governance to promote the economic development of the state.[31]

2.2 Should the Best Law or the Best Man/Woman Rule?

In addition to the question of the relationship between rule by law and the rule of law, another question to be considered regarding the authoritarian governments of the Asian developmental state is whether the rule of man or woman can be an alternative to the rule of law. The authoritarian government which uses law as an instrument to attain the political goals can be conceptually distinguished from the authoritarian (or despotic) government which does not use law at all or pretends to use law only nominally, though, in practice, it is difficult to classify a particular government into either of them.

From the East and Southeast Asian experiences, we can ask why the authoritarian government has so often been needed for development. Can we understand that the authoritarian state is still in a period of transition to the rule of law, and authoritarianism is a necessary condition for establishing strong government through the centralization of political powers? In that sense, is the rule by man/ woman a tentative state on the way to the construction of the rule of law? Or can the rule of best man/woman be an alternative to the rule of law?

---

[30] Matsuo 2009: pp. 53-55.

[31] A typical example is the implementation of industrial policies by enacting the laws to promote certain industries, which have been held important for the state, as mentioned above in the first paragraph in this Sub-section.

It is recognized that effective economic institutions must ultimately be un-dergirded by political institutions that contain the power of the legal enforcement of contracts.[32] Although there is no automatic process to produce political or-ganizations that will create the necessary legal system and precisely enforce it, there are, allegedly, two ideal political models of the authoritarian version and the consensual version: While an authoritarian ruler who sincerely dedicates him/herself to promoting economic growth has a substantial advantage in the short run, in the longer run, a polity based on the consensus of the people in accordance with the rule of law will become dominant. The reason is explained that the ruler's dedication to good economic performance will eventually be un-dermined by unexpected crises and the mortality of the genius rulers. However, not only does the creation of a stable consensual polity, bound by the rule of law, take time[33] but also, more fundamentally, matters to be deliberated in detail and judged promptly cannot be prescribed in law. As a matter of fact, there appeared some successful authoritarian regimes that have shown stable economic growth in the Asian region. Here the discussion comes to the starting point that asks the Aristotelian question of whether the best man or the best law should rule.

But some things can, and other things cannot, be comprehended under the law, and this is the origin of the vexed question whether the best law or the best man should rule. For matters of detail about which men deliberate cannot be included in legislation. Nor does anyone deny that the decision of such mat-ters must be left to man, but it is argued that there should be many judges, and not one only. For every ruler who has been trained by the law judges well; and it would surely seem strange that a person should see better with two eyes, or hear better with two ears, or act better with two hands or feet, than many with many; … These are the principal controversies relating to monarchy.

---

[32] North 2005: p. 118.

[33] North 2005: pp. 157, 161. It requires to develop "a deep underlying set of norms to con-strain players" (ibid.: p. 161).

But may not all this be true in some cases and not in others? For there is by nature both a justice and an advantage appropriate to the rule of a master, another kingly rule, another constitutional rule; but there is none naturally appropriate to tyranny, or to any other perverted form of government; for these come into being contrary to nature. ...[34]

The first paragraph makes critical comments both on the rule of law and the rule of man. The law cannot be comprehensive enough to provide necessary matters, and there are "matters of detail about which men deliberate" and which cannot be included in the law, so they must be left to a person.[35] However, a person cannot see, hear, or act better than many persons.

But the second paragraph implies that there are variations on good government, including monarchy, depending on the nature of the people.

A people who are by nature capable of producing a race superior in the excellence needed for political rule are fitted for kingly government; and a people submitting to be ruled as freemen by men whose excellence renders them capable of political command are adapted for an aristocracy; while the people who are suited for constitutional freedom are those among whom there naturally exists a warlike multitude ... [which is] able to rule and to obey in turn by a law which gives office to the well-to-do according to their desert.[36]

These comments on the rule of law and the rule of man may seem to apply to the development process of Asian countries, which are on the way to rapid economic development. The rule of man/woman still seems to be a rival of the rule

---

[34] Aristotle, *Politics*, Book III, 1287b 16-41 [Barnes (ed.) 1984: pp. 2043-2044].

[35] As for the so-called "third source" of government authority in British-style legal system or the Presidential prerogative in the U. S.-style legal system to act for the public good, when law cannot stipulate in advance what the government should do for the public good, see Waldron 2019: pp. 18-21.

[36] Aristotle, *Politics*, Book III, 1288a 8-15 [Barnes (ed.) 1984: p. 2044].

of law if he/she is full of providence and free from all types of corruption. In the development process, there are so many things to be deliberated by the government, which are difficult to be prescribed in law. In this circumstance, the rule of law is not an absolute value but is the best of the second-best alternatives to the rule of man/woman, who often lacks foresight and is inseparable from corruption.

Not only in the process of development but also in the state of an emergency such as the COVID-19 pandemic, the correct measures that should be taken by the government are difficult to be stipulated by the legislation in advance. Some countries under authoritarian governments seem to manage the epidemic better than other countries, as measured by the number of infected persons and the mortality rate, although there are warnings against excessive surveillance and too strict control of society. Y. Harari puts it:

In their battle against the coronavirus epidemic several governments have already deployed the new surveillance tools. … By closely monitoring people's smartphones, making use of hundreds of millions of face-recognising cameras, and obliging people to check and report their body temperature and medical condition, … authorities can not only quickly identify suspected coronavirus carriers, but also track their movements and identify anyone they came into contact with. A range of mobile apps warn citizens about their proximity to infected patients.

…

Even when infections from coronavirus are down to zero, some data-hungry governments could argue they needed to keep the biometric surveillance systems in place because they fear a second wave of coronavirus, or because there is a new Ebola strain evolving in central Africa, or because … you get the idea. A big battle has been raging in recent years over our privacy. The coronavirus crisis could be the battle's tipping point. For when people are given a choice between privacy and health, they will usually choose health.[37]

---

[37] Harari 2020.

The government of every country has been facing the dilemmas of balancing regulations for public health with guarantees of human liberty. However, it should be noted that there is a governmental success story (such as that of Taiwan), which has thoroughly disclosed the information needed by its citizens according to a special law and created norms for their voluntary cooperation, providing us with a model to balance public health and democratic liberty. It implies that there may be a possible solution to the freedom versus health dilemma, along with the promotion of the rule of law. For that purpose, we need to understand the rule of law flexibly, as a dynamic process to be constructed corresponding to the unique conditions of society.

3. The Construction of the Rule of Law in the Development Dynamics of a State

3.1 The Promotion of the Rule of Law as a Process of Construction of a Building on Preexisting Ground

The rule of law is not a uniform and static entity found in some countries, but rather a diversified and dynamic construction based on the development context of each country. It is like the construction of a building, which will consist of at least three stories to be constructed on the ground as a basis of the building.

First of all, it is important to confirm that the rule of law building cannot be constructed without any preexisting ground on which a new building could be constructed. As for the rule of law building, the ground consists of the existing norms of a society, including traditional norms, customs, beliefs, religions, and other social norms that have been shared by the members of the society and thus are binding. We cannot neglect, ignore, or disregard those existing norms, even though they may seem to be irrational, outdated, or ritualistic. The problem is how to treat them when a new law is introduced in the society.

3.2 The First Floor of the Rule of Law Building

To build the rule of law structure, we have to start from the existing rules, which include the traditionally evolved informal rules; we cannot make a fresh start by removing the existing norms. The new laws, which will either replace the existing rules or amend them, can be introduced by accommodating them in some way. In this respect, the government must pay close attention to the voices of the people about what they think of the current rules and the new laws to be introduced in the society. This is the first floor — the ground floor — of the rule of law construction. The introduction of new laws in a society can be achieved in accordance with the rules to change rules, if any. However, it is often difficult to identify the rules that are used to change rules — the rules of change — in traditional society because traditional rules are not intended to be changed; and if they are changed, the rules of change are not articulated or published.[38] Conflicts may occur when provisions of a new law have some gaps with the existing rules. In this case, it may take time to compromise with the dissenting members of society on the new provisions.

But for the governments of developmental states in Asia, it has been difficult to take enough time to accommodate new provisions with the existing rules, to which changes have been carried out with little delay. Authoritarian governments have often applied new laws with little political pressure from society. In this case, however, the gaps between the new and traditional rules have remained in place for a long time.

3.3 The Second Floor of the Rule of Law Building

Statutory law is not recognized as existing unless it can be applied and enforced in individual cases. The second stage of the rule of law construction is to build the enforcement mechanism to apply the created law to concrete cases and to execute it according to the provisions of the law. In this process, the law

---

[38] The rules to change rules are the secondary rules in the sense of Hart's Concept of Law (see Hart 2012: pp. 95-96). The traditional society does not always have the distinct secondary rules to be distinguished from the primary rules.

should be correctly interpreted and legitimately enforced by the central and local governments, including the courts. In this respect, the government must be both strong and legitimate. It presupposes the centralization of political powers by a country's unified government. This is the second floor of the rule of law building and the stage at which the "rule by law" system can be established, in which the law shall be obeyed by the people as well as by the government.[39] It also conforms to the rule of law in the formal definition.[40]

Through the centralization of political powers, the government must be strong and stable enough to enforce the laws such as those for taxation, for example, and to execute the final judgment of the court. The centralization process, however, differs depending on the historical conditions of each country. Even in the Asian region, this process has significant variation. It should be noted that centralization appears to be a precondition of the rule of law, rather than a result of the rule of law, even though the promotion of the rule of law may support and consolidate centralization, which would ultimately be based on the people's confidence in the government. A centralized and strong government can be compatible with a democratic government, and thus it becomes more stable. A centralized, strong, and stable government should not be confused with a despotic or autocratic government, which is inherently unstable and weak in the long run.

3.4 The Third Floor of the Rule of Law Building

The rule of law will make further progress when it develops the mechanism to regularly review whether the law's content is right and just in accordance with the fundamental principles of the country's basic laws and in consideration of the social change following legislation. Through this progress, the rule of law can advance toward the entity in its substantive definition. This review mechanism can be described as the third floor of the rule of law building.

This mechanism includes a judicial review of the constitutionality of laws

---

[39] As for the element of rule by law, see 2.1 supra.

[40] As for the formal definition of the rule of law, see 2.1 supra.

[Figure] The Rule of Law Building

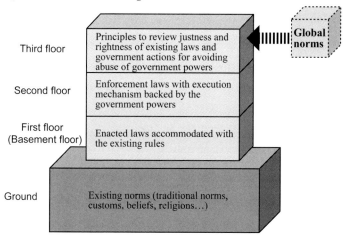

and regulations and of government actions by the normal court and the constitutional court if any. Judicial review, however, should not be enough because the court, including the constitutional court, if any, may be subject to political pressure from the administrative, government party, political parties, and other political groups. The most important and fundamental element of the review mechanism is that the principles to review the content of laws can be analyzed, deepened, and debated so that they reflect the common sense of the society. In this respect, the role of the university is crucial in studying the fundamental principles and methods of dissemination so that they will become articulated and incorporated into people's thoughts.[41]

A vital object of this mechanism is the review of government actions. Through this function, the rule of law should restrain the government from deviating from the law and abusing its powers. In this regard, the rightness and justness of government actions shall be reviewed according to the fundamental principles of law, the power of which should ultimately be based on the people's concern about, acceptance of, and support for them. However, such principles

---

[41] As for the role of university in the rule of law promotion, see 5.2 infra.

are always subject to cross-border debate in a globalizing world; the rule of law construction in one country cannot be isolated from the emerging supranational norms that have developed at the level of the globalizing community of states.

4. The Rule of Law Construction in the Globalizing World

The principles to review the rightness and justness of laws are influenced by the globalization of certain norms. For instance, on 4 September 2013, the Supreme Court of Japan held that Section 900, Item 4, Proviso, First sentence of the Civil Code, which had provided that the inheritance share of an illegitimate child shall be half that of a legitimate child, had been unconstitutional for violating Article 14 (1) of the Constitution[42] when the succession took place for the plaintiff (the illegitimate child) in July 2001 at the latest.[43] It unanimously changed the established precedent, which held on 7 July 1995 that the provision was constitutional, although four judges gave dissenting opinions.[44]

What was the cause of this change to precedent? As is indicated in the reasoning for the judgment, international norms appear to have influenced the decision, including Section 24 (1) and Section 26 of the International Covenant on Civil and Political Rights (1966)[45], and Sec. 2 and Sec. 3 of the Convention on the Rights of the Child (1989)[46]. In addition, Japan received recommendations from the United Nations Human Rights Committee for the elimination of discrimination since 4 November 1993. After this change to precedent, the Diet removed

---

[42] Article 14 (1) of the Constitution of Japan provides: "All of the people are equal under the law and there shall be no discrimination in political, economic or social relations because of race, creed, sex, social status or family origin." The English translation of the Constitution of Japan is available at: [http://www.japaneselawtranslation.go.jp/law/detail_main?id=174].

[43] Supreme Court Decision (Grandl Bench) 4 September 2013 Minji-hanreishū Vol. 67, No. 6, p. 1320 [https://www.courts.go.jp/app/hanrei_en/detail?id=1203].

[44] Supreme Court Decision (Grand Bench) 7 July 1995 Minji-hanreishū Vo. 49, Nor. 7, p.1789.

[45] Japan ratified it on 4 August 1979 and it came into effect on 21 September 1979.

[46] Japan ratified it on 16 May 1994 and it came into effect on 22 May 1994.

Section 900, Item 4, Proviso, First sentence of the Civil Code.[47] The former Section. 900, Item 4, Proviso, First sentence of the Civil Code was based on the principle of respect for legal marriage and protection of marital units. To note is that this principle was neither changed nor abrogated, but rather restricted by the principle of non-discrimination by birth and respect for a child as an individual, which had gradually been diffused into the consciousness of the people.[48]

These globalizing norms are not necessarily "hard laws", ratified and to be enforced by the state such as treaties, but rather "soft laws", which are neither ratified nor enforced by the state, such as the Declaration of the United Nations Conference on the Human Environment (1972), Declaration on the Right to Development (1986), Rio Declaration on Environment and Development (1992), Declaration on the Rights of Indigenous People (2007), Sustainable Development Goals (2015), etc. Similarly, companies can no longer neglect Principles for Responsive Investment (PRI: 2006), which aim to incorporate Environmental, Social, and Corporate Governance (ESG) issues into investment analysis and decision-making processes, Corporate Social Responsibility (CSR) evaluation, Task Force on Climate-related Financial Disclosures (TCFD: 2017), etc. Although these soft laws are not executed by the state, they are actually binding through the concerns of the related parties. In this sense, the rule of law does not mean the rule of hard law which is created and enforced by the state. Current globalizing norms have been woven with hard laws and soft laws to form a complex web of rules created and evolved in the globalizing world. Even national legislation, such as the Civil Code, is within reach of this global web of norms.

An example of this dynamic in Japan is the Law on the Promotion of Policies for Realization of the Society Where the Pride of the Ainu People Shall Be Respected, which passed the Diet on 19 April 2019.[49] Section 1 of this law explicitly

---

[47] Law No. 94, 11 December 2013.

[48] See the concurring opinion by Justice Kiyoko Okabe attached to the court opinion in the Supreme Court Decision (Grandl Bench) 4 September 2013 Minji-hanreishū Vol. 67, No. 6, p. 1320 [https://www.courts.go.jp/app/hanrei_en/detail?id=1203].

[49] Law No. 16, 26 April 2019.

recognizes that the Ainu people are the indigenous people in Japan, the first time so recognized in Japanese legislation. This law was also influenced by the Declaration on the Rights of Indigenous People (2007), together with proposals and activities by global non-governmental organizations.

However, global norms cannot be the legal basis on which the global rule of law shall be constructed, as this would require establishing a centralized world government with united political authority over all states that make up the international system. As I. Kant warned, such a global, centralized world government, either "a universal monarchy"[50] or "a world-republic"[51] would be dangerous because if it abuses its powers or deviates from its laws, there is no higher authority that can effectively restrict it.

The idea of international law presupposes the separate existence of a number of neighbouring and independent states; and, although such a condition of things is in itself already a state of war, (if a federative union of these nations does not prevent the outbreak of hostilities) yet, according to the Idea of reason, this is better than that all the states should be merged into one under a power which has gained the ascendency over its neighbours and gradually become a universal monarchy. For the wider the sphere of their jurisdiction, the more laws lose in force; and soulless despotism, when it has choked the seeds of good, at last sinks into anarchy. Nevertheless it is the desire of every state, or of its ruler, to attain to a permanent condition of peace in this very way; that is to say, by subjecting the whole world as far as possible to its sway. But nature wills it otherwise. She employs two means to separate nations, and prevent them from intermixing: namely, the differences of language and of religion.[52]

---

[50] Kant 1795 (translated by M. C. Smith 1903): Second Section, Second Definitive Article for a Perpetual Peace, p. 155.

[51] Kant 1795 (translated by M. C. Smith 1903): First Supplement, 2, p. 136.

[52] Kant 1795 (translated M. C. Smith 1903): First Supplement, 2, pp. 155-156.

Instead of establishing a world government, either a universal monarchy or a world republic, a system of global governance can be created in which the rule of law building could be constructed in each country as explained above.[53] But, in that system, global norms must be shared by all state members;[54] the system of global governance is destined to fail if each country sticks to a home-country-first policy.

5. The Role of the University in the Rule of Law Construction

5.1 Fostering Legal Intermediaries Who Bridge between Laws and Citizen's Daily Life

In the process of the rule of law construction, the university should play an important role through its education and research activities. As explained above, the principles to review the content of laws and government actions and their effectiveness to restrict government powers could be based on the people's concern about, acceptance of, and support for them. However, the details of legal rules are too complex and technical to be easily understood by ordinary people. They need individuals who can translate technical legal terms into ordinary language and explain complicated legal rules through easy-to-understand examples. An intermediary can provide a bridge between legal matters and citizen's daily life, and whom ordinary citizens can easily access at a reasonable cost. To develop the required number of such intermediaries, the university should provide appropriate curriculums at a reasonable cost within a reasonable period.[55] They will

---

[53] See 3.1 to 3.4 supra.

[54] It can be modeled on "a federation" or "a federative union" in the sense of "an alliance" of nations based on "a covenant of peace" (foedus pacificum) in Kant 1795 (translated by M. C. Smith 1903): Second Section, Second Definitive Article for a Perpetual Peace, and First Supplement, 2, pp. 134, 136, 155.

[55] From this perspective, we should review the legal education programs and the content of state examination or bar examination. Legal abilities to become the intermediary person should be trained in university and measured by examination.

include candidates for judges, prosecutors, and lawyers, and other legal professionals. But that's not all. Graduates of the faculty of law or law-related faculty who do not take or pass the state examination or bar examination to become legal professionals, but find employment in private companies and government offices, can also become intermediaries. The range of persons who can be legal intermediaries could expand through effective legal education. They can include elementary, junior high, and high school teachers who will provide education of law to their students.[56]

Legal education in university has been an academic venture because it aims not only to acquire knowledge of legal rules but also to understand the primary underlying principles through which the meaning of laws, the process of law-making, and the administration of the law can be realized rationally and comprehensively through reflection that coordinates various bodies of legal knowledge.[57]

In order to develop this system of intermediaries who can provide advice for the solution of global issues, not from the narrow view of national interests but from a global perspective, it is worth considering the formation of an international collaborative network among the universities. Pilots of this collaboration among universities to share experiences have already been launched.[58]

5.2 Study of the Rule of Law and Its Promotion

5.2.1 Study Aspects of the Rule of Law

Another role of universities in the rule of law construction is the study of a country's rule of law structure, including traditional norms of the society; the construction process of the rule of law, including the enforcement mechanisms; and the underlying principles, which are the ultimate ground to review the rightness and justness of laws. This study will contribute to identifying impediments

---

[56] As for the education of law for the ordinary people, see 5.3 infra.

[57] See Vinogradoff 1913: pp. 8-9.

[58] The Programs for Fostering Asian Global Legal Professions (PAGLEP) are one of the challenges for that purpose. As for PAGLEP, see [http://keiglad.keio.ac.jp/en/paglep/].

that may hamper the promotion of the rule of law in a country. Obstacles may include the gap between traditional norms and newly enacted laws, which have not been accommodated even after the legislation, the incomplete or immature centralization of the political powers of government, or the change of awareness by society about some principles of laws.

5.2.2 Study of the Structure and Construction Process of the Rule of Law

It should be noted that there would be no uniform rule of law structure because all steps in the rule of law construction must start from existing institutions, which vary greatly from country to country as a part of its governance structure. Therefore, the rule of law must be carefully promoted in conformity with the existing institutions to maintain the governance of each state. The history of Asian countries shows us that efforts by authoritarian governments to change governance by adopting comprehensive new laws have caused confusion and distortions, as well as achievements. In this regard, the historical, socio-legal, and comparative study of the rule of law structure and its construction process in Asian developmental states would be useful. We will find various types of rule of law buildings within the Asian region, with different structures built on different terrain.

At the same time, however, we will also find some similarities in the region as a result of common struggles in the rule of law construction, such as seeking to accommodate the rule of law construction in authoritarian governments with global norms and global legal order.

5.2.3 Study of the Principles Underlying Laws and Government Actions

A crucial aim of legal study is the analysis of underlying principles of laws. It is based on the legal-philosophical analysis of a country's comprehensive legal system by confirming the consistency of laws in conformity with the constitution. However, the object of analysis is not limited to hard laws under the constitution, but also includes soft laws, which are now a part of a country's legal system through the influence of globalizing norms. The study of principles is the normative interpretation of the legal rules that form a country's legal system through reflection. Such an interpretation should also involve an empirical survey of the people's awareness of these legal principles; a serious gap between the principles and the people's awareness and understanding of them, as evidenced by widespread disregard of or disgust with those principles, would hinder a normative force of them as the basis for reviewing laws and government actions.

At the same time, however, the principles and the people's awareness of them are not always perfectly aligned; the gap or tension between them may result from the psychological pressure one feels to follow the principles.[59]

For instance, Article 13 of the Constitution of Japan stipulates: "All of the people shall be respected as individuals. Their right to life, liberty, and the pursuit of happiness shall, to the extent that it does not interfere with the public welfare, be the supreme consideration in legislation and in other governmental affairs."[60] It recognizes individualism in the sense of respecting everyone as an individual as the underlying principle of the Japanese legal system. The meaning of respecting everyone as an individual and the scope of its restriction for reasons of public welfare can be interpreted by considering the normative sense of them in the comprehensive Japanese legal system (including traditional rules and globalizing norms) and the people's awareness of them.

5.3 Making Communication between the Principles and the People's Awareness of Them

If there are a certain gap and tension between the principles underlying the laws and government actions and the people's awareness and understanding of those principles, it is vital for people to make an effort to understand those principles. A better alignment is likely to strengthen people's acceptance of and support for the principles. This is the agenda of education of law to be provided

---

[59] This tense relationship is a natural consequence of providing a norm, which is supposed to guide the people's action by restraining his/her free decision making.

[60] The English translation of the Constitution of Japan is available at: [http://www.japaneselawtranslation.go.jp/law/detail_main?id=174].

to ordinary people.[61] We should recognize that it is a very important and indispensable process of the rule of law construction.[62]

Improving education so that it is provided not only to "gentlemen" but also to a wider circle of people in society, Vinogradoff "would like to explain as briefly and simply as possible the main principles which underlie legal arrangements".[63]

> One need not be a barrister or a solicitor, a member of parliament, a justice of the peace, or even an elector, to take an interest in and feel responsibilities towards laws: all those who pay taxes and own property of any kind, who hire and supply labour, who stand on their rights and encounter the rights of others, are directly concerned with laws, whether realize it or not. Sometimes a knowledge of law may help directly in the matter of claiming and defending what belongs to one; on other occasions it may enlighten a juror or an elector in the exercise of his important functions; in any case, every member of the community takes his share in the formation of public opinion, which is one of the most potent factors in producing and modifying law.
>
> … Although the details of legal rules are complicated and technical, the operations of the mind in the domain of law are based on common sense, and may be followed without difficulty by persons of ordinary intelligence and education.[64]

In the education of law, the legal intermediaries mentioned above[65], including law teachers in universities, are expected to provide not just technical knowledge of the law but also explanations of the underlying principles by using easy-to-un-

---

[61] As for the education of law to be provided by elementary, junior high, and high school teachers for their students, see 5.1 supra. But the education of law is not limited for students but should also be provided for ordinary persons.

[62] Strengthening the people's awareness of underlying principles is a part of the third floor construction in the rule of law building as mentioned above (see 3.4 supra and Figure).

[63] Vinogradoff 1913: pp. 7, 9.

[64] Vinogradoff 1913: pp. 8-9.

[65] As for the legal intermediaries, see 5.1 supra.

derstand terminology in ordinary language for individuals who have had an ordinary education and who may take an interest in and feel a sense of responsibility toward the law.[66] If those principles could be transformed into "common sense" of the people and could create a "public opinion" on crucial occasions, they would become the strongest aspect of the law. In this sense, the method of education of law is a significant object of study to contribute to the rule of law construction.

6. Conclusion: The Asian Challenge for the Rule of Law Ubiquitous World

The rule of law cannot be established in a shorter period of time, and Asian countries are still seeking its promotion. In the process of modernization[67] and independence from colonial rule[68], Asian countries embarked on building the rule of law through the transformation of a governance structure into either a constitutional monarchy or a republic. The first priority on the agenda was the centralization of political powers following the feudal rule or the colonial rule. The second item on the agenda was economic growth to strengthen the financial basis of the state led by the newly-established, but often still centralizing government. The government enacted laws as a measure to implement government policies, which was characterized as rule *by* law. The rule of law in the sense that the law should restrain centralized and strong government power has been demanded by some governments in Asia that are still in the process of centralization. This pressure to promote the rule of law has been increasing in the

---

[66] Different from the legal education, the education of law may be expected to provide for ordinary persons by the legal intermediaries on a volunteer basis.

[67] Since the end of the 19th century, modernaization of Asian countries was promoted by the government officials who studied in and foreigners whom the government hired from European countrie, so that it was mostly Westernization in its substance.

[68] The exceptions were Nepal, Thailand, and Japan.

globalization movement. However, it should be noted that, as the structure and the construction process of the rule of law in Asian countries tells us[69], without the construction of rule *by* law as the first and second floors of the rule of law building, the rule of law would not be established. The construction of the rule of law building in Asian countries is still ongoing. The point is how to combine the strengthening of the government through centralizing political powers with restricting those political powers in order to avoid abuse and irregularities. How can the "law" effectively restrict "politics"? Kant has already taken up this issue.

Now certainly, if there is neither freedom and nor a moral law founded upon it, and every actual or possible event happens in the mere mechanical course of nature, then politics, as the art of making use of this physical necessity in things for the government of men, is the whole of practical wisdom and the idea of law [der Rechtsbegreff] is an empty concept. If, on the other hand, we find that this idea of law necessarily to be conjoined with politics and even to be raised to the position of a limiting condition of politics, then the possibility of reconciling them must be admitted. ...[70]

Kant proposed relying on "a moral politician," who "understands the principles of statesmanship to be such as do not conflict with morals," and who is different from "a political moralist," who "fashions for himself such a system of ethics as may serve the interest of statesmen."[71] We can add the following story by paying attention to the education of law for the people, who can become, foster, or watch "a moral politician," and legal education for the legal intermediaries who will provide the education of law.[72] This is a common challenge of the

---

[69] As for the rule of law's structure and its construction process, see 3.1 to 3.4 supra.

[70] Kant 1795 (translated by M. C. Smith 1903): Appendix I, p. 165. A part of translation is changed in accordance with the original text.

[71] Kant 1795 (translated by M. C. Smith 1903): Appendix I, pp. 165-166.

[72] Also they can become, foster, and watch "a moral politician" for themselves. For the education of law and legal education, see 5.1 and 5.3 supra.

Asian countries that are currently constructing the rule of law. Their experiences will provide useful lessons on how we can use law to manage politics under the unique conditions in each country. They will enrich the general theory of the promotion of the rule of law applicable under different conditions in different countries.

By using these experiences, if the rule of law as described — as a three-story building on the own ground — were constructed in as many countries as possible, and if global governance were established as a federation of peaceful states without creating a world government[73], the rule of law would be enjoyed in many places on the globe. It would contribute to creating a space in which anyone, at any time, and anywhere could enjoy the fair and effective protection of rights and freedoms as a benefit of the rule of law, just like the air we breathe wherever we happen to be on the planet. We can call that space "the world in which the rule of law is ubiquitous" or abbreviatedly "the rule of law ubiquitous world."[74] It is an ideal, which is still far from the present conditions, but it is worth the challenge.[75]

References:

Aristotle, *Politics*, in Jonathan Barnes (ed.), *The Complete Works of Aristotle, the Revised Oxford Translation*, Vol. 2, Princeton University Press, 1984.

Balasubramaniam, Ratna Rueban, "Has Rule by Law Killed the Rule of Law in Malaysia," *Oxford University Commonwealth Law Journal*, Vol. 8, No. 2, 2008, pp. 211-236.

Dworkin, Ronald, *A Matter of Principle*, Harvard University Press, 1985.

---

[73] For the establishment of a sustainable world peace through the formation of a federation of peace (foedus pacificum), see Kant 1795 (translated by M. C. Smith 1903): Second Section, Second Definitive Article for a Perpetual Peace, pp. 134, 136.

[74] For the concept of rule of law ubiquitous world, see [http://keiglad.keio.ac.jp/en/keiglad/].

[75] It will contribute to the realization of inclusive institutions expressed in the Goal 16 of the Sustainable Development Goals (SDGs), which aims to promote peaceful and inclusive societies for sustainable development, provide access to justice for all and build effective, accountable and inclusive institutions at all levels. As for the SDGs, see [https://sdgs.un.org/goals].

Harari, Yuval Noah, "The world after coronavirus," [https://www.ft.com/content/19d90308-6858-11ea-a3c9-1fe6fedcca75], *Financial Times*, 20 March 2020.

Hart, H. L. A., *The Concept of Law*, Third Edition, with a Postscript edited by Penelope A. Bulloch and Joseph Raz, and with an Introduction and Notes by Leslie Green, Oxford University Press, 2012.

Johnson, Chalmers, *MITI and the Japanese Miracle: The Growth of Industrial Policy, 1925-1975*, Stanford University Press, 1982.

Kant, Immanuel, *Zum ewigen Frieden: Ein philosophischer Entwurf*, Königsberg, bei Friedrich Nicolvius, 1795; translated by M. Campbell Smith M.A., *Perpetual Peace: Complete with Introduction, Notes, Supplements, Appendices, and Index*, Wildside Press, 2009.

Li, Ji, "The Leviathan's Rule by Law," *Journal of Empirical Legal Studies*, Vol. 12, No. 4, 2015, pp. 815-846.

Lugosi, Charles, "Rule of Law or Rule by Law: The Detention of Yaser Hamdi," *American Journal of Criminal Law*, Vol. 30, 2003, pp. 225-278.

Matsuo, Hiroshi, "The Rule of Law and Economic Development: A Cause or a Result?," in: Y. Matsuura (ed.), *The Role of Law in Development: Past, Present and Future*, Nagoya University, CALE Books, 2005, pp. 59-70.

Matsuo, Hiroshi, "Let the Rule of Law be Flexible to Attain Good Governance," in: Per Bergling, Jenny Ederlöf and Veronica L. Taylor (eds.), *Rule of Law Promotion: Global Perspectives, Local Applications*, Iustus, Uppsala, 2009, pp. 41-56.

Matsuo, Hiroshi, "Access to Justice in Indochinese Countries," in Michèle and Henrik Schmiegelow (eds.), *Institutional Competition between Common Law and Civil Law*, Springer-Verlag, 2014, pp. 249-277.

Matsuo, Hiroshi, *Hattensuru-ajia-no-seiji-keizai-hō: Hō-wa-seiji-keizai-no-tameni-nani-ga-dekiruka [Politics, Economics and Law in Developing Asia: What Can Law Do for Development?]*, Nihonhyoron-sha, 2016.

Morgenbesser, Lee, *The Rise of Sophisticated Authoritarianism in Southeast Asia*, Cambridge University Press, 2020.

Ng, Kwai Hang, "Is China a Rule-by-Law Regime," *Buffalo Law Review*, Vol. 67, No. 3, 2019, pp. 793-821.

North, Douglass C., *Understanding the Process of Economic Change*, Princeton University Press, 2005.

Peerenboom, Randall (ed.), *Asian Discourses of Rule of Law*, Routledge Curzon, 2004.

Rajah, Jothie, *Authoritarian Rule of Law: Legislation, Discourse and Legitimacy in Singapore*, Cambridge University Press, 2012.

Raz, Joseph, *The Authority of Law: Essays on Law and Morality*, Clarendon Press, Oxford, 1979.

Stephenson, Mattew, "The Rule of Law as a Goal of Development Policy," [https://www.securewebexchange.com/metamodequadrant.com/stephenson.html], 2001.

Silverstein, Gordon, "Singapre: The Exception That Proves Rules Matter," in: Tom Ginsburg and Tamir Moustafa (eds.), *Rule by Law: Politics of Courts in Authritarian Regimes*, Cambridge University Press, 2008.

Studwell, Joe, *How Asia Works: Success and Failure in the World's Most Dynamic Region*, Grove Press, 2013.

Tamanaha, Brian, *On the Rule of Law: History, Politics, Theory*, Cambridge University Press, 2004.

Tushnet, Mark, "Rule by Law or Rule of Law," *Asia Pacific Law Review*, Vol. 22, No.2, 2014, pp. 79-92.

Vinogradoff, Paul, *Common-sense in Law*, Williams & Norgate, 1913.

Waldron, Jeremy, "Rule by Law: A Much Maligned Preposition (25 April, 2019)," *NYU School of Law, Public Law Research Paper,* No. 19-19, Available at SSRN: [https://ssrn.com/abstract=3378167 or http://dx.doi.org/10.2139/ssrn.3378167].

World Bank, *The East Asian Miracle: Economic Growth and Public Policy*, Oxford University Press, 1993.

Chapter 2

THE ROLE OF FACULTY OF LAW, THAMMASAT UNIVERSITY, IN PROMOTING ACCESS TO JUSTICE IN THAILAND DURING THE COVID-19 PANDEMIC

Ronnakorn Bunmee*

(Thammasat University)

1. Introduction

The coronavirus disease 2019 (COVID-19) pandemic hit Thailand traumatically as it did virtually all countries worldwide. To limit the outbreak, the government imposed a lockdown on almost all businesses between March and July 2020. The lockdown measures were intended to prevent a catastrophic health crisis. As a result, there were just 4,261 confirmed cases and 60 deaths[1] against the previous estimate of over 350,000 patients.[2] Therefore, it came as no surprise that the World Health Organization praised Thailand as a "successful model for containing the spread of COVID-19."[3] Conversely, the World Bank anticipated

---

* Assistant Professor, Faculty of Law, Thammasat University.

[1] World Health Organization, WHO Coronavirus Disease (COVID-19) Dashboard, accessed from https://covid19.who.int/ on 18 December 2020.

[2] Faculty of Science Mahidol University, The estimation of the COVID-19 pandemic growth rate, accessed from https://stang.sc.mahidol.ac.th/kb/?p=766, on 18 December 2020.

[3] UN News, Thailand's COVID-19 response an example of resilience and solidarity: a UN Resident Coordinator blog, accessed from https://news.un.org/en/story/

that Thailand's economy would contract significantly to become the worst affected nation in the East Asia and Pacific Region.[4]

In short, Thailand's success in containing the virus's spread has glaringly devastated the country's economy. This economic failure is partly because of the near halting of international tourist arrivals and near cessation of global trade, which are the aorta of Thailand's economy. Thailand relies heavily on international trade and tourism to thrive, so it was evident that the economy would suffer greatly when both dropped. The lockdown measures rubbed salt into the wound since private consumption, especially of retail and recreational services, has practically halted due to these measures. When the economic arteries and capillaries are both blocked, the lifeblood of the economy stops flowing. There are at least two issues concerning debts that have arisen due to a ruined economy and related mobility restrictions. First, many debtors probably cannot meet their obligations. Second, debtors cannot seek quick, reliable legal advice about what they should do when performance is rendered impossible due to their change in circumstances.

The first part of this paper will outline some legal consequences under Thai law when repaying debts is impossible. The next part will explain the role that the Faculty of Law of Thammasat University has played in this dire situation to help people access justice.

2020/08/1069191 on 18 December 2020; ThaiPBS, WHO director praises Thailand as a good model for containing COVID-19, accessed from https://www. thaipbsworld.com/who-director-praises-thailand-as-a-good-model-for-containing-covid-19/, on 18 December 2020.

[4] The World Bank, Thailand Economic Monitor June 2020: Thailand in the Time of COVID-19, accessed from https://www.worldbank.org/en/country/thailand/publication/ thailand-economic-monitor-june-2020-thailand-in-the-time-of-covid-19, on 18 December 2020.

2. Change in Circumstances under Thai Law

There are two sections provided in the Thai Civil and Commercial Code that deal with a situation where performance has been rendered impossible, sections 205, 218, and 219, shown below.

Section 205   If the performance is incomplete due to a circumstance for which the debtor is not responsible, the debtor is not in default.

Section 218   If the performance becomes impossible due to a circumstance for which the debtor is responsible, the debtor shall pay the creditor the compensation for non-performance damages…

Section 219   If the performance becomes impossible due to a circumstance that occurred after the obligation formed, for which the debtor is not responsible, the debtor is relieved from the obligation…

Since this paper discusses the impossibility of performing due to the COVID-19 pandemic, which is not the debtor's fault, section 218 is not applicable. It will not be mentioned again in this paper. The difference between the two remaining sections is that while section 205 deals with temporary impossibility, section 219 deals with permanent impossibility.

These two sections are applied automatically to all contracts unless they include a specific clause that says otherwise. The impossibility of performance can occur as a permanent or temporary impossibility. The difference between the two categories is the potential removal of obstacles leading to the inability to repay the debt. Suppose the debtor, for instance, is a singer contracted to perform in a concert. However, due to government-imposed restrictions on movement and crowd gathering, the debtor cannot perform. This is a case of temporary impossibility since the debtor can still sing at a concert when the restrictions are lifted.

One needs to differentiate between a performance that is impossible to deliver and one that is extremely difficult, which would require the debtor to endure substantial hardship or expense. The latter case still refers to potential performance; thus, the obligation is not excused. Then we shall consider whether the COVID-19 mobility restrictions and economic hardship have rendered performance impossible. To the best of the author's knowledge, there is no direct Supreme Court ruling stating that COVID-19 constituted a *force majeure*. None the less, according to previous precedents, one should not have any difficulties understanding that COVID-19 will be considered a *force majeure* and rendered many contractual performances impossible to deliver. The exact answer to the question depends on the nature of the performance and how the pandemic affected the debtor's ability to perform.

Here are some notable relevant Supreme Court's rulings;
Supreme Court Decision 3546/2546 (2002)[5]

The 1998 Asian financial crisis that caused the collapse of most financial institutions and gross damage to all business sectors in Thailand, and severely affected many debtors' ability to repay the debts owed to financial institutions, did not automatically render the performance impossible. The Court must verify the impossibility of performance on a case-by-case basis to determine whether the debtor is relieved from the obligation without liability.

Supreme Court Decision 2934/2522 (1979)[6]

The debtor agreed to sell construction materials made of crude oil to the creditor. However, an increase in the price of crude oil in the international market led to a sharp increase in the domestic market's construction materials and affected their availability. The debtor refused to perform the obligation on the grounds of the impossibility of performance. The Supreme Court held that it was not an impossibility of performance.

---

[5] Translated by Associate Professor Dr Munin Pongsapan.
[6] Translated by Associate Professor Dr Munin Pongsapan.

3. The Faculty's Role in Promoting Access to Justice: TU Pandemic Legal Aid Center

Since virtually no major legislative changes exist to cope with the COVID-19 pandemic situation, the Faculty, guided by Dean Munin Ponsapan, initiated the TU Pandemic Legal Aid Center[7] to help people, regardless of nationality or financial status, receive legal advice online free of charge. The only criterion was that the client must not be from a for-profit organization as the Faculty offering the service based on charity. This *ad hoc* legal aid center is in line with the university's core values, which holds the rule of law and the people as paramount. It was established with the view that both Thai and foreign people's opportunities to access legal advice has been severely limited due to the restrictions. Without proper knowledge, people are considerably disadvantaged when facing a legal dispute that must be settled.

Since this was an *ad hoc* legal aid center with limited resources, the cases eligible for consultations had to relate to the COVID-19 pandemic. Otherwise, the client could contact the LAW TU Legal Aid Center, which has been established for more than 40 years and still ran concurrently with the COVID-19 legal aid center. In exchange for free legal advice, every client had to provide their consent to the Faculty to publish redacted data relating to their case in the public interest. Up to July 2020, there were 80 cases deemed eligible and thoroughly consulted. Of that number, 55% and 30% were labor cases and contract disputes, respectively; only a little over 10% about criminal matters. Most of the clients (85%) chose to receive consultations through Facebook Messenger.

Besides providing free legal consultations, the TU Pandemic Legal Aid Center also published academic papers about law and the pandemic through online platforms to transfer knowledge and increase outreach. This was implemented in the hope that people residing in Thailand might better understand their rights in the middle of the crisis, therefore reducing the disadvantages suffered

---

[7] For more information of the centre, visit https://www.facebook.com/tulawcovid19.

by vulnerable people.

4. Conclusion

Although 2020 will be remembered as one of the most distressing and difficult years on record, it will also be remembered as one year where people came together to help those in need get through this unprecedentedly tough time. The Faculty of Law, Thammasat University, is proud to serve the community as a source of legal knowledge and the home of leading lawyers working for the country and as one of the beacons of hope for people in need. We will continue to champion more effective legal instruments and lawyers and the equality of all the people before the law.

Chapter 3

ACCESS TO LEGAL INFORMATION:

A Case of Vietnam

Phan Thi Lan Huong*

(Hanoi Law University)

1. Why Access to Legal Information Is Important in Building a Rule of Law State

According to the Oxford English Dictionary, the term "rule of law" is defined as: *"The authority and influence of law in society, especially when viewed as a constraint on individual and institutional behavior; (hence) the principle whereby all members of a society (including those in government) are considered equally subject to publicly disclosed legal codes and processes."*[1] This term is interpreted from the French phrase *la principe de legality* (the principle of legality), which is defined as government based on tenets of law and not the whims of men.[2] *Rechtsstaat* is the term used in German legal and political terminology. The United Nations (UN) refers to "rule of law" as "a principle of governance by which all persons, institutions, and entities, public and private, including

---

* Law lecturer, Deputy Head of International Cooperation Department, Hanoi Law University
[1] Oxford English Dictionary online, See Garner, Bryan A. (Editor in Chief). Black's Law Dictionary, 9th Edition, p. 1448 (Thomson Reuters, 2009).
[2] "Origin and Concept of Rule of Law," accessed August 4, 2020, https://www.lawteacher.net/free-law-essays/administrative-law/origin-and-concept-of-rule-of-law-administrative-law-essay.php.

the State itself, are accountable to laws that are publicly promulgated, equally enforced and independently adjudicated, and which are consistent with international human rights norms and standards."[3] The Association of Southeast Asian Nations (ASEAN) Charter also obliges member states to adhere to the rule of law and to promote and protect human rights and fundamental freedoms.[4]

However, the rule of law is interpreted differently from country to country, depending on political and social conditions. In other words, the concept is transplanted differently in different societies. For example, in common law countries which follow separation principles, jurisdiction of the courts is crucial important, therefore, the judges hold power to interpret the laws and case precedents are important sources of laws. Whereas, in civil law countries, laws are the main sources for resolving disputes. Nonetheless, there are some common elements, such as: "(1) a government bound by and ruled by law; (2) equality before the law; (3) the establishment of law and order; (4) the efficient and predictable application of justice; and (5) the protection of human rights."[5] The rule of law embodies the principle that all people are equal under the legal system and attempts to ensure that everyone is accountable to the law. Put more succinctly, the rule of law means that no one is above the law.

In Vietnam, rule of law is quite a new concept and officially stipulated under the 2013 Constitution: *"The Socialist Republic of Vietnam is a socialist rule of law State of the People, by the People and for the People"*[6] Vietnam has instituted legal reforms intending to build a comprehensive legal system in

---

[3] UN Security Council, The Rule of Law and Transitional Justice in Conflict and Post-Conflict Societies: Report of the Secretary-Genre-al to the Security Council, S/2004/616, 23 August 2004. https://digitallibrary.un.org/record/527647?ln=en, accessed 1 December 2020.

[4] Charter of the Association of Southeast Asian Nations, Chapter I, Article 1 (7).

[5] "Origin and Concept of Rule of Law," accessed August 6, 2020, https://www.lawteacher.net/free-law-essays/administrative-law/origin-and-concept-of-rule-of-law-administrative-law-essay.php.

[6] The 2013 Constitution, Article 2(1).

which human rights are protected and state powers are controlled. Vietnam is in a transitional period, government has made great efforts in developing free market policies. The 2013 Constitution defines the concentration of state power as follows: *"The State powers are unified and delegated to state bodies, which shall coordinate with and control one another in the exercise of the legislative, executive and judiciary powers."*[7] Although, there is no separation of powers or checks and balances between the legislative, executive, and judicial branches in Vietnam, Vietnam under the Communist Party has developed a comprehensive legal framework to provide impartial control of the use of power by the state as a key factor in building a rule of law state. The 2013 Constitution also stipulates that: *"(1) The State is organized and operates in concordance with the Constitution and the law, manages society by the Constitution and the law and practices the principle of democratic centralism; (2) All state agencies, cadres, officials and employees must show respect for the People, devotedly serve the People, maintain close contact with the People, listen to their opinions and submit to their supervision; resolutely struggle against corruption, wastefulness and all manifestations of bureaucracy, arrogance and authoritarianism."*[8]

Like the other developing countries in Asian, promoting rule of law and legal reform are very important conditions for achieving the Millennium Development Goals in Vietnam. Globalization is influencing legal system of Asian countries. It requires each country to reform its legal system towards rule of law and good governance standards. Vietnam has been struggling for building a rule of law state. Socialist rule of law state in Vietnam includes the following features: (1) state power belong to people; (2) distribution of state power; (3) separation of party leading role and state management; (4) development of consistent and stable legal system: (5) effectiveness of law in administration; (6) equal legal protection; (7) and the independent of the judicial system.[9]

---

[7] The 2013 Constitution of Vietnam, Article 2(3).

[8] Ibid., Article 8.

[9] Hongyi Chen, *Constitutionalism in Asia in the Early Twenty-First Century* (Cambridge University Press, 2014), 198.

In addition, human rights are also protected by the Constitution. It is the first time that the term "human rights" has been officially recognized in the Constitution. Article 14 (1) provides that: *"In the Socialist Republic of Vietnam, human rights and citizens' rights in the political, civic, economic, cultural and social fields are recognized, respected, protected and guaranteed in concordance with the Constitution and the law."* According to this article, human rights are protected and guaranteed by the State. In other words, State agencies are responsible for ensuring that all citizens can exercise their rights and enjoy their freedom in all aspects of daily life. Vietnam has embarked on reforming its legal system to ensure detailed implementation of human rights.

Access to information is a fundamental right of the people and plays an important role in building a rule of law state. "The right to access to official documents is considered essential to self-determination of the people and the exercise of the fundamental human rights, while helping administrative agencies appear more legitimate and trustworthy in the public eyes."[10]

Currently, there is a proposal for a UN Convention on the Right of Free Access to Public Legal Information as an independent and substantive right incorporated in the Hague Conference Guiding Principles.[11] The right to access to information is crucial for building an accountable and transparent government, as well as promoting access to justice. It is evident that lack of legal access to information may infringe on human rights or the legitimate interests of individuals and groups. For example, during the COVID-19 pandemic, persons with disabilities and ethnic minorities had difficulties accessing information about allowanc-

---

[10] Hermann-Josef Blanke and Ricardo Perlingeiro, *The Right of Access to Public Information: An International Comparative Legal Survey* (Springer, 2018), 3.

[11] Mitee, Leesi Ebenezer, The New Human Right of Free Access to Public Legal Information and its Proposed United Nations Convention (October 6, 2019). Mitee, Leesi Ebenezer, The Human Right of Free Access to Public Legal Information Book Series, Upcoming Volume 1 (2020), Available at SSRN: https://ssrn.com/abstract=3131610 or http://dx.doi.org/10.2139/ssrn.3131610

es or healthcare services.

Every member country of the UN has to develop a comprehensive legal framework for promoting their citizens' access to justice. The Principles asserts the right of free access to public legal information as a legal right and emphasizes its importance in the international human rights framework. People need access to legal information as one key element for ensuring justice.[12]

Enabling individuals and organizations to access legal information is crucial for promoting accountability and transparency of government. Every government needs to guarantee this right by developing legal regulations and building effective data systems. This is also necessary for citizens to be protected. Access to legal information is also a key element for access to justice. A key challenge for every country trying to build a rule-of-law State is ensuring access to legal information in criminal proceedings, in administrative disposition processes, and in decision-making.

2. Current Situation Regarding Access to Legal Information in Vietnam

The right to information is one of the fundamental human rights guaranteed under the 2013 Constitution: *"Citizens have the right to freedom of speech and freedom of the press, and have the right of access to information, the right to assembly, the right to association, and the right to demonstrate. The exercise of those rights shall be prescribed by law."*[13] Access to information is one of the fundamental rights needed to ensure democracy. In 2016, the National Assembly en-

[12] Beth Bilson, Brea Lowenberger, Graham Sharp, REDUCING THE "JUSTICE GAP" THROUGH ACCESS TO LEGAL INFORMATION: ESTABLISHING ACCESS TO JUSTICE ENTRY POINTS AT PUBLIC LIBRARIES, Windsor Yearbook of Access to Justice, 2017, page 100 https://wyaj.uwindsor.ca/index.php/wyaj/issue/view/479, accessed August 4, 2020.

[13] The 2013 Constitution, Article 25.

acted legislation on access to information to clearly define the term: "Information refers to details and data that are contained in existing documents and papers and stored in writings, printouts, electronic texts, pictures, photos, drawings, tapes, disks, video recordings, audio recordings or in other forms produced by state agencies."[14] This law also laid out the rules for ensuring access to information:

1. All citizens are treated equally and not discriminated against in exercising their right of access to information.

2. The information must be provided in an accurate and sufficient manner.

3. The provision of information must be made in a timely and transparent manner, convenient for citizens to access, and in conformity with procedures regulated by the law.

4. Restrictions on the right of access to information must be regulated by the law, where necessary, for the purpose of ensuring the national defense and security, social security, social ethics, and community health.

5. The exercise of the citizens' right of access to information must not be harmful to national interests, lawful rights, and the interests of other agencies, organizations, and individuals.

6. The Government grants favorable opportunities for the disabled and those who reside in border regions, islands, mountainous regions, and other areas with difficult social and economic conditions, to practice their right of access to information.[15]

The legislation mandates that the following documents must be accessible to the public: administrative documents with universal effect; drafts of legislative documents; national and local socio-economic development strategies, programs, projects, schemes, and plans...[16] Significantly, Vietnam also enacted measures

---

[14] Law on access to information, 2016.

[15] Law on access to information, Article 3.

[16] Law on access to information 2016, Article 17 (see annex).

to ensure that citizens were informed about their legal right to information, with the State having responsibility for such public education initiatives (Article 2). This law also defines the methods of informing citizens about their rights, such as press releases, mass media, loudspeakers, internet, panels, posters, publication in the official gazettes; publishing on government websites; posting in a head office, on the notice boards of agencies, organizations, and residential areas.[17]

Legal information is found in legislative documents, judgments, and administrative decisions. Every legislative, executive, and judicial organizations must provide adequate and free access to its laws and law-related publications.[18] Currently, these documents are stored in a database system, mostly under the 4.0 technology renovation period. The legal information is usually searched through web portals that are maintained by public and private institutions.[19] In Vietnam, there are some portals that provide free access to legal information—the Ministry of Justice; government website, and the Supreme People's Court. However, this is very limited access since the database system has not yet been developed.

Vietnam has carried out administrative reforms to create e-government infrastructure. According to the UN's e-Government Assessment Report in 2016, Vietnam's e-Government Development Index (EGDI) placed the country in 89th place out of 193 countries. This was an advance of ten places over the past two years, with the component index of online public services (OSI) increasing by eight places to reach 74th place (compared to the year 2014.) In 2018, Vietnam's EGDI ranked 88th out of 183 countries, moved up one place, including the online service component index (OSI) which rose by 15 spots to 59 out of 193 countries (compared to the year 2016.) In 2019, the Government of Vietnam issued Res-

---

[17] Law on legal popularization and education 2012, Artilce 11.

[18] Beth Bilson, Brea Lowenberger, Graham Sharp, REDUCING THE "JUSTICE GAP" THROUGH ACCESS TO LEGAL INFORMATION: ESTABLISHING ACCESS TO JUSTICE ENTRY POINTS AT PUBLIC LIBRARIES, Windsor Yearbook of Access to Justice, 2017, page 100 https://wyaj.uwindsor.ca/index.php/wyaj/issue/view/479, accessed August 4, 2020.

[19] Ibid.

olution No.17/NQ-CP which specified the tasks and measures required for the development of electronic government for the period 2019–2020 and up to 2025. This Resolution listed as a key goal the development of a *"system for consultation of policies and legal documents in order to shorten the time to handle work, reduce meetings, reduce administrative paperwork, publicly disclose the process of collecting opinions and improve the quality of drafted legislative documents, special documents and increase the accountability of drafting agencies, putting it into operation in December 2019, and continuing to develop and complete it during the period 2020–2015."* [20] This shows that Vietnam has tried to promote the right to access to legal information through developing e-government. Access to legal information is considered part of "self-help services" and will promote transparency and knowledge of the legal system.[21]

In general, access to legal information is guaranteed in the following areas:

2.1 Access to law enactment

The Law on Promulgation of Legal normative documents (Law on Laws 2015, amended in 2020) requires that draft laws and decisions issued by competent organs must open for public comments before enactment. *"During the formulation of legislative documents, the drafting agencies and relevant organizations must enable other organizations and individuals to provide opinions about formulation of legislative documents and draft legislative documents; seek opinions from entities regulated by legislative documents."*[22] According to this provision, the drafting agencies are responsible for collecting public comments. Currently, drafts of legal documents are often published on the government portal for public comment. The amended Law on Laws 2020 also defines the responsibility of drafting agencies to consider and respond to the comments during the drafting phase.[23] Legal documents may be translated into ethnic languages and

---

[20] Resolution No.17/NQ-CP dated 7 March 2019, IV Major tasks, and solutions, 3 (b).

[21] "Law and Policy Reform at the Asian Development Bank," n.d., 3.

[22] Law on Promulgation of Legal normative documents, 2015, Article 6 (2).

[23] Law on Promulgation of Legal normative documents amended 2020 and comes into force

foreign languages for reference purposes.[24] This provision enables ethnic minority groups or foreigners living in Vietnam to access legal information. However, the number of translated documents is very limited. In addition, the legal documents are published on the portal of the related government agencies. Regarding publishing legislative documents in the Official Gazette, Article 150 lays out the following guidelines:

1. Legislative documents of central regulatory agencies must be published in the Official Gazette of Socialist Republic of Vietnam, except for those that contain state secrets.

2. Legislative documents of the People's Councils and the People's Committees of provinces, local governments of administrative-economic units must be published in the official gazettes of their provinces.

3. Legislative documents of the People's Councils and the People's Committees of districts and communes must be posted publicly and broadcast on local media. Time and location for posting shall be decided by the President of the People's Committee of the district or commune.

4. Within 3 days of the publishing or signing date, the agency or person competent to promulgate legislative documents must send the document to the regulatory of Official Gazette (Vietnam News Agency) for publishing or public posting.

The Vietnam News Agency shall publish the legislative document in full on the Official Gazette within 15 days if it is promulgated by a central regulatory agency or within seven days if it is promulgated by the People's Council or the People's Committee of a province or local government of an administrative-economic unit from the day on which the document is received.

5. Legislative documents published on paper and electronic Official Gazette are official and as valid as the original documents.

---

from January 01, January 2021, Article 2 (amended article 6 of Law 2015).

[24] Law on Promulgation of Legal normative documents, 2015, Article 9.

6. The Government shall provide regulations on Official Gazette and posting of legislative documents.

All this shows that the right to access to legislation is guaranteed in Vietnam. Legal documents can be accessed by different sources, including the web portals of the National Assembly, Vietnamese Government, Ministries, Ministry-level Agencies and the Government's Agencies, local government, as well some websites that focus on specific certain areas of laws. For example, the Vietnam Chamber of Commerce and Industry under the Ministry of Industry and Trade provides free and open access to legal information about business, commerce, and investment, including legal texts and cases.[25] However, the number of such open access websites is quite limited. Currently, there are some database systems that provide these services, such as the Law library website.[26] In addition, official translated legal documents to foreign languages and ethnic minority languages remain as a crucial challenge for Vietnam to ensure all ethnic minority groups and foreigner to access legal information effectively.

2.2 Access to judgments and decision-making by judicial organs

Under the Criminal Procedure Code 2015 or Civil Procedure Code 2015, a trial will be open for participation. For example, Article 25 Criminal Procedure Codes provides that "A Court tries publicly, and every person is entitled to attend the trial, unless otherwise stated in this Law. For special cases involved in state secrets, national traditions, protection of persons aged below 18 or personal privacy as per litigants' rational requests, a Court may try in closed session but must pronounce its judgments publicly." However, access to the Court judgment is still limited. Only the relevant parties can get the judgment from the Court. The laws do not determine clearly the right to access legal information during the

---

[25] Le Thi Hanh, Open Access to Official and Authenticated Legal Information in Vietnam, 2013, Creative Commons Attribution 3.0 Unported License: http://creativecommons.org/licenses/by/3.0/

[26] https://thuvienphapluat.vn/

investigation process. Since 2016, Vietnam has introduced case precedents, with the Justice Council of the People's Supreme Court deciding which cases shall be included in case laws. Those selected case precedents have been published on the website.

2.3 Access to decisions issued by executive organs

During the decision-making process, administrative organs must follow administrative procedures prescribed by laws. However, Vietnam still lacks legislation on administrative procedures that would mandate a public hearing as compulsory procedures in advert disposition. Consequently, people cannot get access to full legal information before issuing decisions. Hence, the number of administrative disputes remains very high in Vietnam. Currently, Vietnam has developed e-government platforms that enable individuals or organizations to access legal information for applications, such as online investment certificate application. The laws on access to information define the responsibility of state agencies to provide information when requested by citizens. Article 10 states that citizens may obtain information through one of the following methods: (1) Exercise the freedom of access to information announced by state agencies; (2) Request state agencies to provide information. *"Information is provided free of charge for citizens, except for other cases of fee collection as regulated by law."*[27] According to this provision, access to information is usually free of charge, but not for all cases. Citizens can access decisions and other information generated by administrative agencies such as the annual reports. However, annual reports are not often disclosed online. In practice, individuals often submit requests to state agencies for annual reports and statistical reports. However, this access is quite limited, since some state agencies are reluctant to share their reports with the public. For example, the Viet Nam Provincial Governance and Public Administration Performance Index (PAPI) 2019 indicated that only 34.3% and 51.7% of respondents indicated that they were, respectively, "Very pleased" and "Pleased" with public

---

[27] Law on access to information 2016, Article 12 (1).

Table: Satisfaction with Public Administrative Services by Accessibility to Information about Procedures, 2019

	Access to Certification Procedures		Access to Construction Permit Procedures		Access to Land Use Rights Certificates Procedures	
	One-stop Shop	Government Portal	One-stop Shop	Government Portal	One-stop Shop	Government Portal
Very Displeased	0.47%	0.13%	0.80%	3.55%	2.54%	2.25%
Displeased	1.80%	1.42%	2.78%	1.07%	7.07%	3.82%
Normal	11.69%	8.30%	16.39%	24.33%	21.15%	17.06%
Pleased	51.73%	47.11%	48.47%	44.23%	45.77%	45.51%
Very Pleased	34.31%	43.04%	31.56%	26.82%	23.48%	31.35%
Mean (5 point scale)	4.17	4.31	4.07	3.90	3.81	4.00

(Source: UNDP, The Viet Nam Provincial Governance and Public Administration Performance Index (PAPI) 2019, page 21)

administrative services by accessibility to information about procedures (see table above).

Significantly, access to decisions issued by administrative agencies is crucial for protecting the rights of individuals and organizations. For example, land acquisition in Vietnam is an enforcement to transfer of land use rights from land users to the government through local administration agencies. Land acquisition decisions are made on several grounds: national defense, public security, or socio-economic developments for the benefit of the nation and the community. In such cases, the land user has no recourse and is primarily concerned about compensation and resettlement. Hence, individuals or organizations need access to information related to land acquisition decisions issued by administrative agencies. It is crucial to ensure the balance of interests among the parties: the government, the investors, and the people whose land is acquired. Such access is also necessary to ensure democracy through exercising the right of supervision of people with seized land.[28]

---

[28] PGS.TS Phan Trung Hien, Quyền tiếp cận thông tin trong thu hồi đất, bồi thường, hỗ trợ, tái định cư - nhìn từ thực tiễn Thành phố Cần Thơ, http://lapphap.vn/Pages/tintuc/tinchitiet.

2.4 Access to free legal aid services

Legal advice and legal aid play an important role in ensuring non-discrimination in the protection of human rights. Legal aid should not cover only the cost of using services, but also the requirement to provide information, advice, mediation, and other support services as judicial or quasi -judicial proceedings.[29] Access to legal aid is also guaranteed by Vietnamese laws. Legislation enables disadvantaged groups to access legal aid services. These groups can obtain legal information in the process of seeking legal redress. However, free access to all information is still limited in Vietnam. Moreover, only a small number of people are eligible for legal aid, hence this is a "justice gap" since many low- and middle-income people cannot pay for legal advice.[30] Under Article 7 of Law on Legal Aid 2017, the only groups who can get free legal aid provided by government are: (1) persons recognized for their meritorious services in the revolution: (2) poor households; (3) children; (4) ethnic minority people permanently residing in exceptionally difficult socio-economic conditions (5) accused persons from between 16 and 17 years of age; (6) accused persons in near-poor households; and (7) poor persons who are elderly, have disabilities, or victims of domestic violence.

2.5 Protection of the right to access to information

To ensure the implementation of the right to access to information, the Law on Access to Information 2016 defines the right to file complaints or lawsuits as follows: The applicant for the provision of information is entitled to complain or file a lawsuit against the relevant state agency or the information provider in the following cases: (1) when competent agencies deny to provide information without reasonable legal grounds; (2) provide information that does not fit the request

---

aspx?tintucid=21044, accessed August 24, 2020.

[29] Council of Europe Committee of Ministers and Council of Europe Steering Committee for Human Rights, *Effective Access to the Law and to Justice for the Very Poor: Recommendation No. R (93) 1 Adopted by the Committee of Ministers of the Council of Europe on 8 January 1993 : And Explanatory Report* (Council of Europe, 1994), 11.

[30] "Law and Policy Reform at the Asian Development Bank," 3.

of individuals; (3) provides insufficient or inappropriate information; (4) does not provide information in a timely fashion.[31]

These complaints or lawsuits will be handled in accordance with Law on Complaint 2011 or Law on Administrative Lawsuit 2015. Individuals or organizations also can claim for compensation of damages. Article 15 of Law on Access to Information provides that: *"(1): Persons who commit acts of violation against the access to information law shall, depending on the nature and severity of their violations, be disciplined or face administrative penalties or criminal prosecution as regulated; (2) If the information provider commits any of prohibited acts stated in Article 11 of this Law and causes damage, the state agency in charge of providing information must provide compensation and the individual who has such act of violation must assume reimbursement liability as regulated by the law on state compensation liability."*[32] The administrative procedures must be disclosed to the public and everyone can access and follow all procedures of application for a permission/certificate since, if an individual does not know about procedures, he/she cannot fulfill his/her rights. For example, A applies for a land used right certificate but, after an inordinate wait, still has not yet received any information from the relevant agencies, yet fails to file a complaint about the delay. His complaints centers on the act of not issuing the land used right certificate, but not the act of not providing information.

3. Conclusion

Access to legal information has played important role in the protection of human rights and building a rule of law State. Access to legal information enables citizens to know their rights and access the judicial system to seek legal redress. Legal information is a key element of information and access to information is

---

[31] Law on Access to Information 2016, Article 14, Article 34.
[32] Ibid., Article 15.

recognized as a fundamental right of citizens. Vietnam has developed a legal framework to ensure the right to access to legal information through many areas, including law–making, decision-making, and judicial proceedings. Access to information promotes transparency and accountability of governments as one of the standards of good governance. Hence, government has to ensure that citizens can exercise their rights without any obstacles or barriers. In other words, the government should eliminate all barriers that prevent people from access to information and ensure all information directly affecting the rights and interests of citizens is made public.

The Government of Vietnam plans to create an e-Government platform to improve the effectiveness and efficiency of the state administrative apparatus and the quality of service rendered to people and businesses. The goal is to develop e-Government based on data and open that data in a Digital Government. Vietnam aims to become one of the top four ASEAN countries in the e-Government ranking by 2025.[33] Hence, developing e-government is crucial for promoting access to legal information by individuals and organizations. To promote the rights access to legal information as one of the key factors for promoting access to justice, Vietnam needs to focus on the following measures:

(1) Public participation in the decision-making process should be guaranteed by laws. Government should not only bear responsibility for creating open forums/channels for public participation, but should also determine the legal liability of relevant agencies in responding to public comments. For example, the laws should mandate the decision-drafting organs to respond to public comments in written form which explains clearly the reasons for adoption or rejection of public comments. If the agencies cannot provide a reasonable explanation for their adoption or rejection, people can file a complaint or bring them to Court.

(2) To develop a data-based system that provides open access to all legislative

---

[33] Resolution No.17/NQ-CP 2019.

documents and decisions issued by relevant agencies. All these legislative documents and regulations must translated into English for reference, since foreign enterprises and individuals living in Vietnam need to know about Vietnam's legal system.

(3) To increase the number of people who qualify for access to legal aid services. For example, while victims of domestic violence have such access, other people who are at high risk of violence, such as sex workers, do not. Hence, the law on legal aid should be revised to enable all disadvantaged groups access to free legal aid services. In addition, the government should also provide other support services during judicial proceedings. Government is responsible for eliminating all barriers that prevent people from access to legal information—for example, providing signed language interpreters for deaf people, or referring victims of sexual abuse to the healthcare system for treatment and collecting evidence.

(4) The Law on Access to information should be revised to ensure that all annual reports of state organs should be disclosed publicly. This will promote accountability and transparency in government. Access to official documents helps to increase people's trust and enables them to monitor government's activities.

(5) Public hearings should be made compulsory procedures in the decision-making of administrative agencies. Participation in decision-making will enable individuals and organizations to contribute their ideas and opinions about policies that directly affect their rights and interests. Such participation also promotes transparency and accountability of government and prevents government from making decisions based on group interests instead of the public interest.

In brief, access to legal information enables people to know about their rights and seek for legal redress. Legal information are disclosed to public is a value of democratic society because it makes government more accountability and transparently. It also promotes equality before laws because people can participate in law – making, decision – making process that ensure laws and decisions respond to public interests. Access to legal information should be recognized as a fundamental right and promoting effective mechanism to ensure the rights to access legal information is one of key element for building rule of law state.

4. References

The 2013 Constitution

Law on legal popularization 2012

Law on Promulgation of Legal Normative Documents 2015, amended in 2020

Law on Access to information 2016

Beth Bilson, Brea Lowenberger, Graham Sharp, REDUCING THE "JUSTICE GAP" THROUGH ACCESS TO LEGAL INFORMATION: ESTABLISHING ACCESS TO JUSTICE ENTRY POINTS AT PUBLIC LIBRARIES, Windsor Yearbook of Access to Justice, 2017, https://wyaj.uwindsor.ca/index.php/wyaj/issue/view/479

Charter of the Association of Southeast Asian Nations, Chapter I, Article 1(7).

Le Thi Hanh, Open Access to Official and Authenticated Legal Information in Vietnam, 2013, Creative Commons Attribution 3.0 Unported License: http://creativecommons.org/licenses/by/3.0/

Mitee, Leesi Ebenezer, The New Human Right of Free Access to Public Legal Information and its Proposed United Nations Convention (October 6, 2019). Mitee, Leesi Ebenezer, The Human Right of Free Access to Public Legal Information Book Series, Upcoming Volume 1 (2020), Available at SSRN: https://ssrn.com/abstract=3131610 or http://dx.doi.org/10.2139/ssrn.3131610

Origin And Concept Of Rule Of Law," accessed August 6, 2020, https://www.lawteacher.net/free-law-essays/administrative-law/origin-and-concept-of-rule-of-law-administrative-law-essay.php

Oxford English Dictionary online, See Garner, Bryan A. (Editor in Chief). Black's Law Dictionary, 9th Edition, p. 1448 (Thomson Reuters, 2009).

UN Security Council, The Rule of Law and Transitional Justice in Conflict and Post-Conflict Societies: Report of the Secretary-Genre-al to the Security Council, S/2004/616, 23 August 2004.

5. Annex

Law on access to information, 2016.

Article 17. Information subject to mandatory disclosure

1. The following types of information must be disclosed publicly:

a) Legislative documents; administrative documents with universal effect; international treaties of which the Socialist Republic of Vietnam is a member or international agreements to which Vietnam is a signatory; administrative procedures and working procedures of state agencies.

b) Information regarding the dissemination and guidance on the implementation of laws and policies in sectors under the state management.

c) Drafts of legislative documents as regulated by the law on promulgation of legislative documents; contents and results of the referendum and acquisition of people's opinions about issues which are under the decision of state agencies and have to be asked for people's opinions as regulated by the law; schemes and their drafts on the establishment, dissolution, merger or division of administrative units or modification of administrative areas;

d) National and local socio-economic development strategies, programs, projects, schemes and plans; sector/field planning, methods and results thereof; annual working programs and plans of state agencies.

dd) Information regarding state budget estimates; reports on state budget enactment; state budget statements; estimates, enactment reports, statements of budgets of fundamental construction programs/projects funded by state budget; state budget procedures.

e) Information regarding the provision, management and use of official development assistance (ODA) and non-governmental aid as regulated; information about the management and use of social relief and benefits; and information about the management and use of people's contributions and types of funds;

g) Information about lists of public investment and public procurement projects/programs, and the management and use of public investment funding, the situation and results of the execution of public investment plans/programs/projects; bidding information; information on land use plans; land price; land appropriation; plans for compensation, site clearance and resettlement concerning regional projects/works;

h) Information about investment activities funded by state budget, the management and use of state capital in enterprises; reports on business and ranking of enterprises; reports on the supervision of the disclosure of financial information of enterprises and state agencies representing owners; information about the organization and operation of state-owned enterprises;

i) Information about products, goods and services that have adverse influence on the health and environment; inspection conclusions in the fields of environmental protection, community health, foods safety and labor safety.

k) Information about functions, tasks, powers and organization structure of agencies and their affiliated units; tasks and powers of officials in charge of dealing with people's issues; internal regulations and rules promulgated by state agencies.

l) Periodical working reports; annual financial statements; information about the statistics on sectors under the state management; sector/field-related national database; information regarding the recruitment, use and management of officials and public employees; information about lists of scientific programs/topics and results thereof;

m) The list of types of information subject to mandatory disclosure as regulated in Point b Clause 1 Article 34 of this Law; name, address, telephone number, fax number and email address of the state agency or the official in charge of receiving information requests;

n) Information concerning public interests and community health.

o) Information concerning taxes, fees and charges.

p) Other information that must be disclosed as regulated by the law.

2. Apart from types of information prescribed in Clause 1 of this Article, state agencies shall, depending on actual conditions, actively disclose other information that they generate or manage.

Chapter 4

THE RULE OF LAW IN LAO PDR:

Problems and Perspectives

Reginald M. Pastrana*

(Luxembourg Agency for Development Cooperation)

1. Introduction

The Lao PDR has a long history written in the Lao people's struggle through the years to build an independent and prosperous country. The nation adopted its first Constitution in 1991 and amended it in 2003 and 2015 meet the changing needs of socioeconomic development, as well as regional and international cooperation and integration.

The Constitution clearly establishes a political system that reflects that the Lao PDR is a people's democratic state; all powers belong to the multi-ethnic Lao people and are exercised by the people and for their interests. The Lao people's rights as masters of the country are exercised and guaranteed through the political system they chose based on their right to self-determination, which the people expressed by electing a National Assembly whose members represented their rights, powers, and interests.

The administrative system of the Lao PDR consists of the organs of state powers, namely, the National Assembly, the government itself, the people's

* Chief Technical Advisor (LAO/031) Luxembourg Agency for Development Cooperation (LuxDev).

courts, and the People's Prosecutor Offices. There are also newly established provincial assemblies tasked with drawing policies, overseeing the activities in their respective jurisdictions, and representing their local constituents on varied local issues and concerns. In addition to these formal organs, the Lao Front for National Construction organizes mass sociopolitical and professional organizations such as the Lao Federation of Trade Unions, the Lao People's Revolutionary Youth Union, the Lao Women's Union, the Federation of Military Veterans, and others to unite and mobilize the Lao people of all social strata in carrying out the tasks of protecting and developing the country and protecting its citizens' rights and legitimate interests.

2. The President of the State

The President of the State is the head of state of the Lao People's Democratic Republic and the representative of the multi-ethnic Lao people both within the country and abroad.[1] The President of the State is also the head of national defense and national security and the general of the armed civilian army for independent protection, democracy, defending the homeland, and securing the peace and stability of the nation.[2]

The President of the State is elected by the National Assembly by two-thirds vote of all members present,[3] and the term of office of the president is the same as that for the National Assembly:[4] The president can remain in office for not exceeding two consecutive terms.[5] The president has a vice-president who is also elected by two-thirds vote in the National Assembly.[6] The vice-president exe-

---

[1] Article 66, Chapter VI of the Lao PDR Constitution (2015).

[2] Article 66, Chapter VI of the Lao PDR Constitution (2015).

[3] Article 67, Chapter VI of the Lao PDR Constitution (2015).

[4] Article 67, Chapter VI of the Lao PDR Constitution (2015).

[5] Article 68, Chapter VI of the Lao PDR Constitution (2015).

[6] Article 68, Chapter VI of the Lao PDR Constitution (2015).

cutes all tasks assigned by the president and acts on the president's behalf when the president is occupied on other matters.[7] In the event that the President of the State is unable to continue performing duties and responsibilities, the vice-president assumes the role until the National Assembly elects a new president.[8]

3. The Government: The Executive Branch

The government is the executive branch of state powers, administering in a unified manner the State's duties in the political, economic, and sociocultural fields, including national defense and security and foreign affairs. The government consists of the prime minister, deputy prime ministers, ministers, and chairmen of the ministry-equivalent organizations.[9] The government's term of office is the same duration as that of the National Assembly;[10] members can remain in the same position not exceeding two consecutive terms of office.[11]

The prime minister is the head of the government and represents the government in leading and managing the work of the government and local administration, having rights to appoint, transfer, or remove the vice-minister, the deputy head of ministry-equivalent, head of division, deputy head of division, and head of sectorial; appoint or remove provincial governors and the Vientiane governor on the approval of the provincial representatives meeting; and propose promotions and demotions for generals, colonels, and other high-ranking national defense and security officials.[12] The deputy prime ministers are assistants to the prime minister and execute the tasks assigned to them by the prime minister,[13]

---

[7] Article 68, par. (2), Chapter VI of the Lao PDR Constitution (2015).

[8] Article 66, par. (3), Chapter VI of the Lao PDR Constitution (2015).

[9] Article 71, Chapter VII of the Lao PDR Constitution (2015).

[10] Article 71, par. (2), Chapter VII of the Lao PDR Constitution (2015).

[11] Article 71, par. (2), Chapter VII of the Lao PDR Constitution (2015).

[12] Article 72, Chapter VI of the Lao PDR Constitution (2015).

[13] Article 73, Chapter VI of the Lao PDR Constitution (2015).

who may assign particular deputies to carry out duties on his behalf.[14]

The government of the Lao PDR consists also of 14 ministries and two ministry-equivalent organizations; the local administration is composed of 16 provinces and the capital city of Vientiane, 143 districts, and 8,955 villages. The ministers and ministry-equivalent organizations disseminate and implement resolutions of the National Assembly and the government; supervise, monitor, and audit all tasks performed by divisions under their jurisdictions; and coordinate and participate in signing agreements and treaties with foreign countries as approved by the government.[15] However, the National Assembly may pass a vote of distrust on the government or any member of the government provided that the vote is issued by the National Assembly Standing Committee or by the votes of more than one-fourth of the National Assembly total members.[16] In the case that the National Assembly files for distrust of the government or any individual member, the president reserves the right to request that the National Assembly reinvestigate and reconsider such cases case or approve the resignation of the member.[17]

4. The Judicial Branch

The People's Court is the judicial branch of the state.[18] It is the only entity with the right to examine and review cases within the Lao's People Democratic Republic,[19] processing cases through a circuit of trial courts, appellate courts, and the Supreme Court.[20] The People's Court of the Lao's PDR is composed of the People's Supreme Court, local people's courts, and military courts as spec-

---

[14] Article 73, Chapter VI of the Lao PDR Constitution (2015).

[15] Article 74, Chapter VI of the Lao PDR Constitution (2015).

[16] Article 75, Chapter VI of the Lao PDR Constitution (2015).

[17] Article 75, par. (2), Chapter VI of the Lao PDR Constitution (2015).

[18] Article 90, Chapter X of the Lao PDR Constitution (2015).

[19] Article 90, Chapter X of the Lao PDR Constitution (2015).

[20] Article 90, Chapter X of the Lao PDR Constitution (2015).

ified by the law.[21] In necessary cases, the court may be summoned based on the approval of the National Assembly Standing Committee.[22]

The People's Supreme Court is the highest judicial organ of the State,[23] and the people's courts make collective decisions on lower court cases.[24] In their adjudication, judges must be independent and must strictly comply with the laws,[25] and final court judgments are to be respected by all organizations and individuals including the mass sociopolitical organizations; all organizations and individuals are expected to implement any court judgments.[26] The vice-president of the People's Supreme Court is appointed or removed by the president of the state,[27] and judges of the People's Supreme Court as well as the president, vice-president, and judges of appellate courts are appointed or removed by the National Assembly Standing Committee.[28]

The Office of the Supreme Public Prosecutor of Lao People's Democratic Republic is an organization that supervises the implementation of laws with respect to protecting rights and benefits for individuals in society through prosecution of wrongdoing including calling witnesses and defendants in accordance with the law.[29] The Office of the Public Prosecutor is composed of the Office of Supreme Public Prosecutor, the offices of local public prosecutors at provincial and city levels, and the office of the military prosecutor as the law permits.[30] The Office of the Supreme Public Prosecutor supervises the activities of the public prosecutor offices.[31] The deputy supreme public prosecutor is appointed or removed by the

---

[21] Article 91, Chapter X of the Lao PDR Constitution (2015).

[22] Article 91, Chapter X of the Lao PDR Constitution (2015).

[23] Article 92, Chapter X of the Lao PDR Constitution (2015).

[24] Article 92, Chapter X of the Lao PDR Constitution (2015).

[25] Article 94, Chapter X of the Lao PDR Constitution (2015).

[26] Article 98, Chapter X of the Lao PDR Constitution (2015).

[27] Article 93, Chapter X of the Lao PDR Constitution (2015).

[28] Article 93, Chapter X of the Lao PDR Constitution (2015).

[29] Article 99, Chapter X of the Lao PDR Constitution (2015).

[30] Article 100, Chapter X of the Lao PDR Constitution (2015).

[31] Article 101, Chapter X of the Lao PDR Constitution (2015).

president of the state.[32]

5. The Legislative Branch

Under the Constitution of the Lao PDR, the National Assembly plays a vital role in government; it is described as a great institution because its members are directly elected by the people and thus represent their hopes and aspirations. In its role, the National Assembly is the highest policy-making organ of the state. Its collective acts formulate sound policies; promote peace, order, and national reconciliation; provide or provide for health, housing, and education services; alleviate poverty, and protect the nation's environment. Indeed, the National Assembly's collective effort at law-making helps shape the national welfare.

Other than its law-making, oversight, and representation functions, the National Assembly also has pervasive and diametrically executive powers in the affairs of the government: to elect or remove the president and vice-president of the state; to consider and approve the proposed appointment or removal of the prime minister; to consider and approve the organizational structure of the government and the appointment, transfer, or removal of members of the government; to elect or remove the president of the People's Supreme Court and the Supreme Public Prosecutor; and to decide on the establishment or dissolution of the ministries, among others.

In 2015, the Lao PDR introduced some amendments to its Constitution, particularly to establish the provincial assemblies in all provinces and in the capital. It was also decreed that the National Assembly through its Standing Committee would establish the National Electorate Committee to ensure credible elections. The Lao PDR National Assembly was to be at the center of the operations to establish the local provincial councils to shape important local policies; the aim was the effective decentralization and devolution of some social services

---

[32] Article 102, Chapter X of the Lao PDR Constitution (2015).

directly to the local populace. Given this expectation, the government organ took paramount importance, and after the difficult years of protracted civil war, the National Assembly is now in the mainstream, enjoying peace and providing vital reforms to lead the Lao PDR onward to progress and development. At the forefront of that work was the newly established provincial assemblies. The assemblies are the law-making bodies of the local governments in Lao PDR as well as of the capital. As legislative bodies, they are authorized to formulate a limited range of public policies and local laws; members also represent their respective local constituents and oversee the various activities of the local governments under their respective jurisdictions.

6. The Rule of Law and Access to Justice: Some Challenges

In general, the rule of law in Laos is in a fledgling state, particularly in the area of access to justice, although the country has made remarkable progress through the span of time. As the Lao justice system is entering a significant phase, it offers citizens numerous options for legal recourse when their rights are violated. The Government of Laos (GoL) has instituted a strong legal enabling environment to promote law and expand the Lao people's access to justice. Notably, GoL adopted Prime Minister (PM) Decree No. 77 to establish legal aid offices. Currently, the government is attempting to upgrade the village mediation committees (VMCs), local, nonformal justice systems, into a PM decree as well.

LuxDev Project LAO/031 is helping the governance program of Lao PDR through its "Promoting the Rule of Law and Improvement of the Legal Education – Phase 2" project in which LuxDev, together with the support of the Institute for Legal Support and Technical Assistance (ILSTA), assists the GoL to address key capacity and structural gaps that limit the effectiveness of the justice system actors and that inhibit inclusive participation in rule of law reform initiatives, including legal education, law enforcement, and access to justice. To bridge the gap between Lao citizens and the justice system, Project LAO/031 has already established 5 provincial and 15 district legal aid offices around the country. These offices rely on trained district and provincial Ministry of Justice (MoJ) officers, together with members of the Lao Bar Association, to educate their fellow citizens about their legal rights and how to defend their rights in Lao's formal and informal justice systems. While the rule of law in Laos is still in its fledgling state, the project has already gained significant milestones: Last year, LAO/031 was able to support the establishment of four legal aid provincial offices in the provinces of Bokeo, Luang Namtha, Bolikhamxay, and Khamouane, and this year, it is determined to complete the establishment of 15 district offices in 5 targeted provinces: Bokeo, Luang Namtha, Vientiane, Bolikhamxay, Vientiane Khamouane.

7. The Legal Education Campaigns

Using a variety of public education materials including comic books, pamphlets, and multimedia CDs, Project LAO/031 together with the ILSTA supported the various government functionaries, especially the MoJ, to spread information on access to justice, particularly for women and children, to schools, provinces, districts, and villages. Important laws were also disseminated and explained such as against human trafficking and other violations of human rights, land rights, and several others. The Clinical Legal Education program at the Faculty of Law and Political Science (FLP) of the National University of Laos, together with some members of the bar association, provide free legal consultations. They also provide legal referrals and information on human rights and other forms of legal assistance

However, many people, especially women, do not know their legal rights or how to use the formal justice system. Additionally, many do not know where to turn when they face legal problems that could be resolved through the courts or community mediation. To reach the greatest number of vulnerable Lao citizens, the FLP teams held a mobile legal clinic outreach mission in the far-flung province of Attapeu; many citizens were able to attend and receive information on their legal rights, obtain one-on-one counseling, on specific issues and in some cases, request for a competent lawyer to represent them in court litigations.

8. Capacity Building Programs

It must be noted that the Lao People's Supreme Court, the State Inspection Authority, the Office of the Supreme People's Prosecutor, the MoJ, and security sector institutions are critical actors in enforcing the rule of law, increasing security, and protecting citizens' rights. However, they are still not operating at their full capacity, and their authority is still not fully developed. These roles need for further improvement.

To address some of these issues, Project LAO/031 together with ILSTA and in partnership with the GoL's justice institutions is undertaking a broad set of activities in the area of justice sector capacity building and modernization. The primary goal of the program is to support the Lao's justice institutions to strengthen their capacity with the ultimate purpose of improving the rule of law in Laos. Activities include developing capacity in the officers of these justice institutions including focused training on key legal developments such as anti-money laundering and anti-human trafficking efforts.

9. Access to Justice in Lao PDR: Some Perspectives

A strong and reliable justice system in Laos is key to a secure society and a growing economy. The success of our society relies in large part on the trust we all put in the rule of law and the knowledge that the courts will be there to enforce our rights should something go wrong. PM Decree 77 on Legal Aid aimed to increase access to justice for disadvantaged and vulnerable people in Lao PDR, and Project LAO/031 now aims to improve the implementation of the decree. Specifically, the project aims to ensure that people on low income, certain senior citizens, people with disabilities or mental illness, persons without legal capacity and their guardians, orphaned children and their guardians, and children in institutional care all have better access to legal services and that their civil rights are better protected. Publicly funded legal services and other forms of free legal advice and assistance are targeted effectively, and, as a result, increasing numbers of disadvantaged and vulnerable Laotians are pursuing legal services to protect their civil rights.

The project has improved access to justice for many marginalized community members through legal aid services, raised awareness of legal rights among nearly 17,915 people (include viewers on social media), and built the capacity of 3,622 legal practitioners, legal educators, and key players in the government sector. Through ILSTA, the project has enhanced professional development for both women and men in the legal sector by providing legal skills trainings, and the project significantly invested in improving the quality and reach of legal aid services to ensure justice for the poorest and most vulnerable people.

In this vein, the project and its government counterparts are currently developing a legal aid "toolkit" to guide legal aid practitioners and drafting a manual for the VMCs. In one of the training workshops on legal aid and VMCs, Ms. Manichanh Chanthavilay, officer of the MoJ Judicial Promotion System Department and individual in charge of the legal aid program, said that in Khamoune province, the legal aid has benefited already 71 cases for citizens who appreciated the free legal assistance on vital matters such as human trafficking and land disputes.

Project LAO/031 has also promoted the rule of law and protected human rights in Laos, while supporting the judicial system to better serve and address the needs of its citizens. The team worked alongside key government stakeholders to implement reforms and rendered technical assistance and capacity-development support to provincial legal aid offices. Among the reforms it supported was institutionalizing PM No. 77 and holding campaigns to increase awareness of the new law and of the amendments to the VMC legislation to enact them through a separate PM decree. Lately, the project is providing support to institute vital reforms through amending the court enforcement of cases. Responding to the prevalence of human trafficking and money laundering, the project, through the cooperative effort of ILSTA, conducted several seminar-workshop series and offered technical support on how to combat these crimes and assisted the Lao PDR in complying with its agreements with other countries on mutual legal assistance.

Chapter 5

DEVELOPMENT OF ADMINISTRATIVE LAW AND THE RULE OF LAW IN LAOS

Latdavanh Donkeodavong*
(National University of Laos)

1. Introduction

This paper describes the link between administrative law (in the form of state compensation and administrative case litigation) and the overall role that law plays in the concrete state of the rule of law in Laos. For this, it is important to consider the general ideal of the rule of law to indicate how it is connected to state compensation (also known as state liability, redress, or remedy) and litigation of administrative cases, as Laos does not have fully established versions of these systems.[1]

The idea of the rule of law is a central consideration in development policies

* Deputy Head of Research and Academic Service Division, Faculty of Law and Political Science, National University of Laos. Doctor in law, Graduate School of Law of the Nagoya University, Japan. The author would like to express sincere gratitude to the Keio University Law School. The author is also grateful to reviewers whose comments were valuable in this paper. All shortcomings and any errors are assumed full responsibility by the author.
[1] This paper uses the term "state compensation." In Japan, state compensation can be translated as "state redress." It could be found in the Japanese Law Translation Database System for State Redress Act of 1947 (*Kokka Baisho Ho*). See http://www.japaneselawtranslation. go.jp/?re=2.

at the present time.[2] A state that is under the rule of law, its agencies, and its public servants are generally liable for illegal acts or inaction. If the population cannot seek remedies or enforce their rights, the rule of law is undermined.[3] In principle, the basic conditions of the rule of law are respected, protected, and guaranteed by the present Constitution in Laos.[4] In practice, the right of the citizen to bring tort claims in court against the State for financial compensation does not exist. This system involves a special type of tort liability arising from inaction (also known as omission or the non-use of regulatory power), wrongful acts, or negligent lack of use of public authority by the State. The legal system in Laos does not provide the ability to bring litigation against the State. Judicial review of administrative action in the interest of protecting the fundamental rights of the citizenry has not been established, and the administration has greater power than the judiciary. This makes it extremely difficult to litigate against the State due to the lack of standing to bring suit against it.

Laos has been actively implementing reform of its administrative law system following the issuance by the Ministry of Justice and other ministries of the "Master Plan on Development of the Rule of Law in the Lao P. D. R" in 2009. In 2019, the National Assembly established a specialized Chamber of the Administrative Court to adjudicate administrative cases. Following a resolution of the National Assembly's Resolution, the People's Supreme Court has also been drafting an "Agreement on Organizational Structure and Activities of the Chamber of Administrative Courts." The Ministry of Justice likewise has been working on a "Presidential Decree on Administrative Case Proceedings" and a Law on State Compensation. These systems are based on the Master Plan on the Rule of Law.

---

[2] David M. Trubek, "The 'Rule of Law' in Development Assistance: Past, Present, and Future," in *The New Law and Economic Development. A Critical Appraisal*, ed. David M. Trubek and Alvaro Santos (Cambridge: Cambridge University Press, 2006), 74.

[3] William Lucy, "Access to Justice and the Rule of Law," *Oxford Journal of Legal Studies* 40, no. 2 (2020): 378.

[4] Chapter IV (Arts. 34–51) of the Constitution guarantees the Fundamental Rights and Obligations of Citizens.

The State, aid agencies, and inter-university cooperation systems are also promoting the rule of law. The universities are among the key institutions that are promoting the rule of law as part of inter-university cooperation and academic research.

This paper, which demonstrates administrative law reform, the role of law in the rule of law, and the promotion of this concept in Laos, is divided into five parts. Part one contains the introduction. Part two offers an account of the development of administrative law in relation to a newly proposed system of state compensation and administrative case litigation under the rule of law. The third part presents the connection between administrative law and the rule of law in Laos, along with its promotion. Part four concentrates on the lack of access to legal sources and the lack of academic research. The final part provides the conclusion.

2. Development of Administrative Law in Laos

2.1 Historical Development

This part reviews the history of administrative law in Laos from 1975–2014. Laos adopted the Soviet judicial system in 1975,[5] in which the State was a centralized system, similar to those seen in China and Vietnam. At the point when the socialist State was established, administrative law was virtually non-existent, and from 1975 to 1990, there was no Constitution.[6] State functions were based on the policies of the Lao People's Revolutionary Party (hereinafter Party) and was largely ruled by administrative decrees and orders, with no existing legislative procedure.[7]

---

[5] Martin Stuart-Fox, *A History of Laos* (Cambridge: Cambridge University Press, 1997), 168–169.

[6] Government of Laos, "Constitution of Lao PDR," accessed November 28, 2020 http://laogov.gov.la/pages/Constitution.aspx?ItemID=56&CateID=3.

[7] Ministry of Justice et al, "Master Plan on Development of the Rule of Law in the Lao P. D. R Toward the Year 2020" (Ministry of Justice, Office of the Supreme People's Prosecutor,

The first step of basic legislative referendum for Laos was taken with the convocation of the first nationwide People's Representative Congress.[8] The administration also issued Prime Minister's Decree, No. 53/PM, October 15, 1976,[9] which established three branches of state power. First, the legislative power inhered in the People's Supreme Assembly (presently National Assembly). Second, executive power was placed in the government. Last, judicial power was in the People's Courts.[10] Three other basic acts were the Establishment of the Council of Ministers, No. 100, July 30, 1978; the Establishment of the People's Supreme Assembly and Local Administration, No. 101, July 31, 1987; and the Establishment of the Council of Ministers, No. 01/80/SPA, August 10, 1982. These laws were issued in the form of Prime Minister's decrees and orders, along with the Resolution of Local Administration.[11]

Laos was ruled by administrative fiat and had no parliamentary body.[12] It did not recognize any legal precedent or democratic parliament, but only the rule of the Party. No separation of powers seen. The three branches worked together to form a centralized system.[13] The judiciary was part of administration, appointed by the Ministry of Justice.[14] The system of the judiciary was founded on the policies of the Party and administrative instructions.[15] The judiciary and

People's Supreme Court and Ministry of Security, August 2009), 4.

[8] National Assembly, "Brief History of the National Assembly," accessed November 30, 2020 http://www.na.gov.la/index.php?r=site/detailcontent&id=9&left=103.

[9] Boupha Phongsavath, *The Evolution of the Lao State*, 2nd ed. (New Delhi: Konark Publishers, 2003), 121.

[10] For more details of the People's Supreme Court and lower courts, see http://www.peoplecourt.gov.la/la/1/1-2.html.

[11] Ministry of Justice et al., "Master Plan on Development of the Rule of Law in the Lao P.D.R Toward the Year 2020," 8.

[12] Marcus Radetzki, "From Communism to Capitalism in Laos: The Legal Dimension," *Asian Survey* 34, no. 9 (1994): 799–800.

[13] Michael Bogdan, "Legal Aspects of the Re-Introduction of a Market Economy in Laos," *Review of Socialist Law* 17, no. 1 (1991): 107–108.

[14] Phongsavath, *The Evolution of the Lao State*, 121.

[15] The present Constitution in Article 3 declares "the rights of the multi-ethnic people to be

the administration applied re-education the violators of the law as part of justice, based on their traditional system, in the absence of a constitution or overall
system of law.[16] In October 1978, the State enacted an unpublished regulation
which it then developed so that civil and serious criminal offenses would be tried
by the People's Provincial Courts and District Courts (abolished or converted to
the present People's Regional Courts). However, civil liability and petty crimes
were handled at the village level.[17] At the village level, the village chief (*Naiban*
in Lao) and mediators mediated both small civil liability and petty crime.[18] Most
conflicts were not dealt by the People's Courts, but by Village Mediation Units.[19]
Village level was an important factor in Laos.[20]

In 1986, the government introduced its New Economic Mechanism (at the
same period as the *Doi-Moi* [Renovation] in Vietnam).[21] This transition offered
opportunities for the development of administrative law. The State began from
nothing, lacking a Constitution or laws. On March 26, 1989, the People's Supreme Assembly Second Legislature elected its members and became the Constitution Drafting Committee. On August 14, 1991, the first Constitution was
promulgated (later amended in 2003 and 2015) by the sixth ordinary session of
the People's Supreme Assembly Second Legislature.[22] It acknowledged the elements of a state governed by law[23] and called for "rule by law of the people, by

---

the master of the country are exercised and ensured through the functioning of the political
system with the Party as its leading nucleus."

[16] Bogdan, "Legal Aspects of the Re-Introduction of a Market Economy in Laos," 108.

[17] Ibid.

[18] Radetzki, "From Communism to Capitalism in Laos: The Legal Dimension," 804–805.

[19] Ibid., 804.

[20] Ian G. Baird, "Village Law in the Lao Context," *International Institute for Environment
and Development* (2000): 11.

[21] UNDP et al., *Development Finance for the 8th National Socio-Economic Development
Plan and the Sustainable Development Goals in Lao PDR* (Vientiane: UNDP, June 2016), 20.

[22] National Assembly, "Brief History of the National Assembly."

[23] Constitution of the Lao People's Democratic Republic, art. 10 (1991).

the people, and for the people."[24]

A number of laws were passed.[25] The Law on the Government was enacted in 1995 (amended in 2003 and 2016) while the Law on Local Administration passed in 2003 (amended in 2016).[26] Nevertheless, no legal act, law, or regulatory act regarded the state liability of administrative authority. Certain provisions of the Constitution of 1991 (Arts. 56–64) and the laws mentioned above declared the administrative power of the central and local governments. The government was determined to implement the "duties of State in all fields: political, economic, cultural, social, national defense and security, and foreign affairs."[27] These activities sometimes led to disputes between the citizens and administrative agencies. Beginning with economic reform in 1986, the government concentrated on economic development. Much investment was placed on dams and mining. Land disputes arose between the State and private persons. In some cases, a state-owned enterprise or a joint investment project between the state and private sector impacted the life or health of local people.

In these cases, victims of administrative actions faced extreme difficulty in suing the enterprise responsible due to the government's involvement. To deal with such cases, the Prime Minister's Office issued its Decree on Compensation and Resettlement, No 192/PM, July 7, 2005 (amended in 2016). This Decree, however, was unclear and did not cover compensation for prejudice arising in public administration, criminal proceedings, or civil proceedings, as well as the enforcement of the Criminal Court agreement and Civil Court decisions. Indeed, the ordinary courts had no power to deal with administrative cases. The con-

---

[24] Article 2 of the 1991 Constitution declared "all powers are of the people, by the people and for the interests of the multi-ethnic people of all strata in society with the workers, farmers and intellectuals as key components."

[25] Radetzki, "From Communism to Capitalism in Laos: The Legal Dimension," 805.

[26] Government of Laos, "Government considers to approve a number of draft law amendments in November," accessed December 2, 2020 http://laogov.gov.la/activities/pages/press.aspx?ItemID=57.

[27] Constitution of the Lao People's Democratic Republic, art. 56.

trolling administrative actions were weak due to a weak judiciary, poorly trained judges, and lawyers, and corruption involved. The administration had more power than the judiciary as well. Thus, it was very difficult for victims to bring suit against the State.

2.2 Present Situation

This part reviews the developments in administrative law in Laos from 2015 to the present day. The Lao government has the power to deal with all fields related to the State.[28] Recently, the government has focused on economic growth. The building of dams, mining, railways, and highways has accelerated, which has resulted in positive developments. However, the life and health of citizens have been impacted, as has the environment.

According to Japan International Cooperation Agency (JICA), many companies in Laos pollute water resources, which impacts people's health.[29] The World Health Organization also reports that the lives and health of many Lao people have been adversely impacted by economic developments.[30] In the current state of affairs in Laos, victims have few means of obtaining recompense for their harms. The legal system does not recognize litigation against the responsible entities because they are in part run by the State. The government has significant power in Laos. No judicial review of administrative action is possible, so all such avenues are closed.

Laos has recently been pursuing a reform to its system of administrative law. On February 7, 2019, the National Assembly Standing Committee issued Resolution No. 15/NASC to establish a Chamber of Administrative Court. This special Chamber Court will increase managerial capacity, force more responsibility on administrators for government actions, perform public duties, and to protect the

---

[28] Law on the Government, art. 3 (2016).

[29] JICA, *Profile on Environmental and Social Considerations in Lao P.D.R.* (Vientiane: JICA, December 2013), 3–1.

[30] WHO, "Heath and Environment," *WHO*, accessed November 20, 2020 http://mobile.wpro. who.int/laos/topics/environmental_health/en/.

rights of all citizens.[31] The Chamber of Administrative Court is to adjudicate cases of contract or tort claims distinct from those applied in private law. The Chamber Courts are in the People's Supreme Court, Central People's Court, and Capital People's Court.[32] After the establishment of the Court, the National Assembly Standing Committee appointed the Chamber's President of Administrative Court on September 25, 2019.[33]

Since its establishment, however, no legal acts on organizational structure and activities of these Chambers have been issued. Currently, the administration of Laos is drafting the "Presidential Decree on Administrative Case Proceedings." This Draft Decree provides important elements of administrative law to protect the interests of public and support the rule of law.[34] The People's Supreme Court has also been drafting its "Agreement on Organizational Structure and Activities of the Chamber of Administrative Courts." This Draft Agreement has five chapters. Chapter I (Arts. 1–2) provide for the Status and Roles of this Chamber Court while Chapter II (Art. 3) considers the Personnel Structure of the Chamber of Administrative Courts. The Rights and Duties of the Courts are declared in Chapter III (Arts. 4–10). Chapter IV (Art. 11) and Chapter V (Arts. 12–14) describe the Pattern of Its Works and Final Provisions. According to Article 4 of the Draft Agreement, the Central People's Court will decide administrative case proceedings in the first instance. The Central People's Court will decide appeals from decisions at the first instance as an appellate court (or second instance), and

---

[31] People's Supreme Court, "Draft Presidential Decree on Administrative Case Proceedings," (People's Supreme Court, latest revision February 27, 2020), art. 1.

[32] National Assembly Standing Committee, "Resolution on Establishment of the Chamber of Administrative Court", no. 15 (National Assembly Standing Committee, February 7, 2019), art. 1.

[33] National Assembly Standing Committee, Resolution on Appointment the Chamber's President of Administrative Court, no. 155/NASC (National Assembly Standing Committee, September 25, 2019), art. 1.

[34] People's Supreme Court, "Draft Presidential Decree on Administrative Case Proceedings," art.1.

the Chamber of Administrative Court in the People's Supreme Court will have jurisdiction to review on cassation appeals from the decisions of the appellate court.[35]

The establishment of these special Chamber Courts entails significant support for administrative reform in Laos. This system allows citizens to file lawsuits against the public servants to allege mistreatment or inappropriate exercise of administrative power and regarding any carelessness or negligence in serving the public. Many legal disputes regarding land, the environment, public payment, hospital treatment, and other public services have arisen, but no lawsuits can be heard because there has been no body that has jurisdiction or a relevant legal framework for financial compensation.[36] After the establishment of the Chamber Court, it will be possible to litigate administrative cases. The Ministry of Justice has drafted its "Law on State Compensation." This Draft Law is "to ensure the prejudiced persons received proper compensation from the State" and to protect "the legitimate rights and interests of citizens and organizations."[37] Section 1 (Arts. 8–14) of the Draft Law allows filing suit only to an individual and not to an administrative agency or the State.

Administrative case litigation and state compensation systems are important developments for Laos to allow it to protect the rights and interests of its citizens. Under the socialist regime, the State is centralized, and the separation of powers dose not exists. The administration currently has more power than the judiciary. Judicial power is weak, and is serves the administration. No idea of judicial review has been established to review administrative actions. Instead, the judiciary

---

[35] People's Supreme Court, "Draft Agreement on Organizational Structure and Activities of the Chamber of Administrative Courts," (People's Supreme Court, latest revision October 27, 2020), art. 4.

[36] Somsack Pongkhao, "Laos to Establish Administrative Courts," *Vientiane Times*, July 19, 2017.

[37] Ministry of Justice, Draft Law on State Compensation, (Ministry of Justice, latest revision March 3, 2020), art. 1.

followed Party policies and administrative interventions. Whether it is set up as an administrative court, judicial power is important to review the administrative activities. In a possible future for the judiciary of Laos, an ordinary court would also be able to deal with administrative questions, as is done in Japan and other countries. If a state agency makes an error in the course of its administration, such as an incorrect administrative decision or a wrongful act, a court should have the power to review and order such state agency to respond to this or pay for financial compensation. Laos has recently committed to becoming a rule of law State. If this is to be accomplished, Laos must guarantee judicial independence to ensure the lawfulness of administrative actions.

3. Rule of Law and Its Promotion in Laos

3.1 Rule of Law Situation

The rule of law is of central importance and is considered a key dimension in good governance.[38] Different thinkers define the rule of law in a large variety of ways.[39] One broader sense of the rule of law is that it refers to "a set of laws that people in a society must obey and everyone is subject to the rule of law."[40] It is also broadly linked to constitutionalism, separation of powers, and judicial review.[41] All state organizations and their public officers, including the legislature,

---

[38] For more details of the rule of law, see Maurice Adams et al., *Constitutionalism and the Rule of Law: Bridging Idealism and Realism* (Cambridge: Cambridge University Press, 2017). Paul Gowder, *The Rule of Law in the Real World* (Cambridge: Cambridge University Press, 2016).

[39] Harvard Law School is provided a broadly concept of the rule of law. See https://orgs.law.harvard.edu/ruleoflaw/what-is-the-rule-of-law/.

[40] Cambridge Dictionary, "Rule of Law," accessed November 20, 2020 https://dictionary.cambridge.org/dictionary/english/rule-of-law. For more senses of this word, see Bryan Garner (Editor in Chief), Black's Law Dictionary, 11th ed. (Thomson Reuters, 2019).

[41] C. I. Ten, "Constitutionalism and the Rule of Law," in *A Companion to Contemporary Political Philosophy*, ed. Robert E. Goodin, Philip Pettit, and Thomas Pogge (Wiley-Blackwell,

the executive, administrative agencies, and law courts, are required to follow legal prescribed procedures and observe the guarantees of individual rights.[42] This is also the condition under which all members of society, including political leaders, accept the authority of the law.[43] This perspective describes limitations to the powers of political authorities and administrators and those of the governing elite. Under the idea of the rule of law, the state, its agencies, and its public officers are considered responsible for violations of the Constitution or any other law.[44] This is ultimately part of the national effort to become a Rule of Law State.

The rule of law in Laos is closely tied to economic reform. Rule of law was broadly declared as an ideal in Article 10 of the first Constitution of 1991 and again in the same Article of the present 2015 Constitution: "the State manages the society through the provisions of the Constitution and the laws." "Party and state organizations, the Lao Front for National Construction, mass organizations, social organizations, and all citizens must function within the bounds of the Constitution and the laws."[45] Rule of law gained influence in Laos after it appeared as the guiding objective for the development of the rule of law, as announced by the Resolution of the VIII Part Congress.[46] The Resolution of the Party marked Laos's official commitment to becoming a Rule of Law State, in terms of its adoption of the 2009 Master Plan on Development of the Rule of Law in the Lao PDR Toward the Year 2020. This Master Plan calls for the Lao State to respect the rule of law in terms of a State administered "through the Constitution and Laws."[47]

2017), 493.

[42] Almon Leroy Way, "Constitutionalism, and the Rule of Law," accessed December 1, 2020 https://www.proconservative.net/CUNAPolSci201PartTwoB3.shtml.

[43] Oxford Dictionary, "Rule of Law," accessed November 20, 2020 https://www.oxfordlearnersdictionaries.com/definition/english/law#rule_idmg_17.

[44] Leroy Way, "Constitutionalism, and the Rule of Law."

[45] Constitution of the Lao People's Democratic Republic, art. 10 (2015).

[46] Ibid. The 8th Congress of the Party was held in Vientiane Capital from March 18–21, 2006.

[47] Ministry of Justice et al., "Master Plan on Development of the Rule of Law in the Lao P.D.R Toward the Year 2020," 1.

The central idea of this concept is to "secure the extension of ownership of Lao and ethnic people, rights of citizens, rights and interests of children, equality between men-women, ethnic groups, as well as for ensuring the implementation of obligations under international treaties to which Laos is party."[48]

To become a Rule of Law State, the legal system must be connected with the fundamental principles of the Article of the Constitution. The implementation of these principles requires the Constitution and Laws to become supreme legislation. The effective implementation of such legislation requires Laos to develop its mechanisms, political system, and the establishment of law-implementation agencies. All State agencies and their civil servants must perform in accordance with the Constitution and Laws of Laos.[49] Almost all laws are open for administrative interpretation in opposition to the intentions of the legislators. They have often been drafted by administrative bodies, especially by the Ministry of Justice. Constitutional rule, however, designates that the final interpreter of the law is the National Assembly Standing Committee (as an administrative body), not the People's Courts.[50] According to Article 56 of the Constitution, the National Assembly Standing Committee has the legal power to remove the President and Vice President of the People's Supreme Court. This makes for a system that is weak in terms of the rule of law.

The development of the rule of law in Laos is currently being supported by many international organizations. JICA is supporting the project for "Promoting Development and Strengthening of the Rule of Law in the Legal Sector in Lao PDR," which is to support "legal and judicial sector acquire abilities to study legal theories, to implement and enforce basic laws on legal theories and to improve laws and practices (...) as well as the trainer and lecturers of legal education and training sector acquire abilities to train high quality legal practition-

---

[48] Ibid., 2.

[49] Ibid.

[50] Articles 56–57 of the Constitution prescribe the rights and duties of the National Assembly Standing Committee.

ers."[51] The first history of the Lao Civil Code was supported by JICA. The Civil Code was approved by the National Assembly on December 6, 2018 (in effect from January 18, 2019).[52] This is coincident with the "Citizen Engagement for Good Governance, Accountability and the Rule of Law" (CEGGA), funded jointly by the EU, Germany, and Switzerland.[53] Similar projects include the UNDP's Strategic Support to Strengthen the Rule of Law in Lao PDR" (3S-ROL) and the Asia Foundation's "Law and Justice" Program. Both of Luxembourg's Rule of Law projects: the Luxembourg Development Cooperation Agency (LuxDev), LAO/031 project entitled "Support Project to Legal Teaching and Training and to the Promotion of the Rule of Law Concept in Lao PDR" and Inter-University Cooperation Project (University of Luxembourg) are dedicated to strengthening the rule of law through higher legal education. These international organizations are playing the significant roles in supporting the rule of law in Laos.

3.2 The Promotion of the Rule of Law

This section regards the promotion of the rule of law in Laos by legal institutions and Faculty of Law and Political Science (FLP) of the National University of Laos (NUOL) in particular. Since 1994, this legislation has discussed in many sources. Legal data and information have been published through libraries, publication of law books, and the official websites of State agencies. The National Assembly has passed many in this area and published items on in its own official website. The Ministry of Justice and other agencies have also published statutes on their official websites. The official Lao Gazette is the most updated legal website in Laos. Legal acts, laws, and regulatory acts have been published in Lao, and there are growing official and unofficial translations of these legal sources

---

[51] JICA J-ROL Project, "Project Summary," accessed November 30, 2020 https://www.jica.go.jp/activities/issues/governance/portal/laos/ku57pq00002khhw3-att/leaflet_eng.pdf.

[52] JICA, "JICA's Long-Term Law Drafting Support Contributes to Establishment of First Ever Civil Code in Lao," accessed December 2, 2020 https://www.jica.go.jp/English/news/field/2018/- 190327_01.html.

[53] CEGGA has currently been supporting the Lao Draft Law on State Compensation.

into English, although translation in general is still limited. Furthermore, legal developments are described in newspapers and magazines, as well as on radio and television and in other media.[54]

Education in the legal sector was identified by the 2009 Master Plan as a necessary part of building the legal system. To become a judge, public prosecutor, or lawyer, a candidate must graduate from a law school. Universities are a main State institution. They play a significant role in developing the rule of law due to the improvements they bring to the legal system and training competent judges, public prosecutors, and attorneys. One of the main law schools in Laos is the FLP. It was created by the Ministry of Justice in 1986 and then was integrated into NUOL and renamed the FLP. It recently operates under the supervision of the Ministry of Education and Sports.[55] It has benefited by international assistance to promote the rule of law through the Swedish International Development Cooperation Agency on "Strengthening Legal Education and Training in Lao PDR," beginning in 2000. It was replaced by the first LuxDev (LAO/23) and then by present LuxDev (LAO/031) in the "Supporting Project to Legal Teaching and Training and to the Promotion of the Rule of Law Concept in Laos." The University of Luxembourg is also filling the gaps through an inter-university cooperation for the development of legal research at the FLP. Lecturers from the University of Luxembourg lecture on important legal topics for Laos and its transition toward a Rule of Law State.

The FLP is cooperating with many State organizations to promote the rule of law, such as the National Assembly, the Ministry of Justice, the People's Courts, Public Prosecutors, and Law Schools in the North, Center, and South of the country. Indeed, it is also cooperating with many universities across the world, including the Japanese universities Nagoya University and Keio University Law School, the University of Luxembourg, Umeå University (Sweden), University of

---

[54] Ministry of Justice et al., "Master Plan on Development of the Rule of Law in the Lao P.D.R Toward the Year 2020," 36.
[55] Ibid., 27.

Lyon (France), and Hanoi Law University (Vietnam). Five universities in Thailand, Thammasat University, Chulalongkorn University, Chiang Mai University, Mahasarakham University, and Mae Fah Luang University, are also cooperating.[56] This internal and external cooperation with both has improved knowledge and the quality of teaching over the last two decades.

The FLP is now the best Law School in Laos. Many lecturers are working at a high level of quality. A large number of external lecturers from the Ministry of Justice, People's Courts, and Public Prosecutors are also delivering lectures. Many law lecturers have been involved in drafting laws, including the Civil Code and Penal Code. However, the promotion of the rule of law has not been straightforward, and many challenges remain to be overcome. The quality standards of FLP are far behind those of Western university and ASEAN standards. Its development will take time and must proceed step by step.

4. Lack of Access to Legal Sources and Academic Research

4.1 Lack of Access to Legal Sources

The basic conditions of the rule of law are accessibility, publicity, and access to justice.[57] Article 38 of the Constitution guarantees the fundamental rights of citizens to "receive education, research, knowledge, and skill development." This Article appears to include the right to legal information. At the heart of the concept of the rule of law is citizens' capacity to access legal information and materials from state agencies. Accessibility is a main issue for scholars and law students as they conduct legal research and draft their reports.

---

[56] Faculty of Law and Political Science, National University of Laos, "External Cooperation," accessed December 2, 2020, https://flp.nuol.edu.la/.

[57] Perrine Simon, "The Role of Law in the Rule of Law, the Contribution of Academics in Lao PDR," *KritV Kritische Vierteljahresschrift für Gesetzgebung und Rechtswissenschaft* 102, no. 3 (2019): 217.

While legal information is currently much more available in Laos than it was, it remains limited and not up to date. The People's Supreme Court has published a small number of judgments on its own website.[58] The lower courts, however, do not have their own websites, and their judgments are not public. It is a challenging task to do legal research in Laos. When a researcher or law student needs to read a judgment, an official letter must be sent requesting it. There is no centralized database of judgments and no statistics available on how many cases are decided by the courts per year. Secondary sources include a limited range of legal studies, law books, law journals, reports, and other materials.

Many State agencies have overlapping legal acts, laws, and other regulatory acts, and they are not systematically published. According to the Master Plan on the Rule of Law, there are four main weaknesses in legal information. First, "legal information center has not been effectively and systematically developed and the service is not widely and timely." It is also not established broadly. Second, the provision of legal data and information is insufficient and cannot meet public demand. Third, "budgetary support, funding to develop legal data and information, and dissemination law are not sufficient enough." Finally, dissemination through mass media is not done according to any plan, and there is little a variety of Law dissemination, and it is not effectively suitable to the target group."[59] There is also no e-Library system among State agencies, with the exception of the FLP.

It seems that it would be difficult to promote the rule of law in Laos. Sources of legal and judicial data must be systematically developed step by step, based on the State of the Rule of Law. Dissemination of information to the people creates the conditions necessary to secure the ownership of rights and justice, which, in turn promote the effective implementation of and respect for the laws. This is necessary to ensure the development of legal information in a systematic and modern manner.[60]

---

[58] See for more details of the People's Courts, http://www.peoplecourt.gov.la/la/.

[59] Ministry of Justice et al., "Master Plan on Development of the Rule of Law in the Lao P.D.R Toward the Year 2020," 36–37.

[60] Ibid., 37.

4.2 Lack of Academic Research

Legal research is an important function of universities around the world. However, it has been limited in Laos due to low lecturer qualifications. Many lecturers at Lao Law Schools have recently completed their bachelor's degrees, while some have master's degrees. The FLP has a large number of lecturers with master's degrees, and some with doctoral degrees. However, the majority of lecturers "lacked adequate numbers of lecturers and all are required lecturers with more experience in the role law plays in the market economy."[61] There are some legal researchers, and many lecturers are from the field of political science.[62] However, there are some researchers on the doctoral level. The low level of qualified lecturers and the weak academic qualifications are severe restrictions on the development of research activities.[63]

The government has been promoting academic research. A new grading system for teaching staff was introduced by the government in the late 1990s and was then replaced with the "Decree on Teacher Academic Positions in Higher Education Institutions," No. 03/GO, January 10, 2020. This system includes four categories of university lecturer: Professor, Associate Professor, Lecturer, and Assistant Lecturer.[64] This enables teaching staff to conduct academic research. After this point, legal research has increased in Laos, but it remains low quality.

Most academic studies conducted by lecturers are not to high-quality standards and are not in the field of law. Most lecturers do not clearly understand the distinction between law and political science; in particular, what is implied for research. Many lecturers have understood legal research to be field research in

---

[61] Ibid., 27.

[62] Seven lecturers have currently completed doctoral degrees at the FLP, but only two of them are in the field of law, including the author while other lecturers are in the field of political science and education management.

[63] Bourdet, *Strengthening Higher Education and Research in Laos* (Stockholm: Sida, 2001), 14.

[64] Government of Laos, "Decree on Teacher Academic Positions in Higher Education Institutions," no. 03/GO (Government of Laos, 2020), art. 5.

interviews and collected qualitative data. In general, the conception of legal research clearly refers to black letter research, using primary sources (statuses, treaties, and cases) and secondary sources (doctrine), such as law books and law journal articles. Lecturers and law students are thus often unable to analyze law properly. They are not encouraged to develop independent or creative thinking, and their legal memoranda and examination are not conducted in a scientific way.[65]

Various forms of inter-university cooperation are ongoing at present. The University of Luxembourg, along with the LuxDev Project (LAO/031), supports the FLP's academic staff. This cooperation has the intention of building legal knowledge and academic law research. This has taken the form of supporting legal research by providing a grant for a short research stay at the University of Luxembourg and publishing a paper in English in a law journal.[66] Some lecturers are conducting research in cooperation with other foreign universities as well. This will help improve the qualifications of the lecturers for doing legal research and allow them to approach common international standards in the future.

5. Conclusion

Laos is developing into a Rule of Law State. Under the rule of law, constitutionalism, separation of powers, judicial review, and court protection must be recognized. Judicial review must be established to enable administrative actions to be reviewed. The court must have the power to order administrative agencies to exercise its legal authority. The rule of law is linked with state compensation and administrative case litigation. Illegal actions or inaction by the State, its agencies, or its public servants must entail the payment of compensation. A rule

---

[65] Simon, "The Role of Law in the Rule of Law, the Contribution of Academics in Lao PDR," 215.

[66] Ibid., 216.

of law state cannot be established without legal guarantee for individual rights. The State has been reforming its administrative law system by in the Presidential Decree on Administrative Case Proceedings and Law on State Compensation. However, the statutes face some problems about financial compensation and judicial power.

Another basic condition of the rule of law involves accessibility, publicity, and access to justice. Accessibility to legal information is limited in Laos. Judgments and law are in no way systematically published. Therefore, it is difficult for researchers and law students to find legal sources. Law books, law journals, and other legal materials are also of limited availability. Most law lecturers have low quality standards. The studies conducted by law lecturers are often of low quality. It is difficult to access to legal sources, which limits academic legal scholarship. Because international organizations and inter-university cooperation are supporting its development, legal institutions in Laos have been improved and are promoting the rule of law. However, this requires time and is a long-term goal.

In sum, Laos is positively pursuing its goal of becoming a Rule of Law State. The strengthening of its legal system and the promotion of the rule of law are supporting academic research. Law school is the main institution where good legal research is being conducted, and this can be used to improve the legal system. Therefore, Laos must be invested in legal institutions and continue to cooperate with inter-university initiatives to achieve its goal. This requires time and effort, and it must be done step by step.

Chapter 6

LEGAL ASPECT ON CHILD'S RIGHTS IN MYANMAR

Khin Phone Myint Kyu*
Khin Khin Su**
(University of Yangon)

1. Introduction

In Myanmar culture, the welfare of children is always the chief priority in society. Myanmar acceded to the Convention on the Rights of the Child on July 15, 1991, with reservation on Articles 15 and 27 and became State Party to the Convention on August 14, 1991. Myanmar now endeavors with utmost effort to implement the Convention in accordance with its sociocultural context and legislative systems. Because Myanmar is a member of the United Nations Convention on the Rights of the Child, the Myanmar Child Law[1] was promulgated on July 14, 1993, and the reservations were withdrawn on October 15, 1993. However, Child Law 1993 was repealed by the *Pyidaungsu Hluttaw* (the Union Parliament) in 2019, and it enacted the Child's Rights Law on July 23, 2019. Among child rights, the most important, such as survival and development, non-discrimination, best interest, and protection, will be discussed in this paper. These rights can be seen

---

* Dr, Professor, Department of Law, University of Yangon.
** Dr, Lecturer, Department of Law, University of Yangon.
[1] The State Law and Order Restoration Council Law No. 9/1993.

in the 2008 Constitution, the Child's Rights Law, Myanmar Customary Law, the Penal Code, the Civil Procedure Code, and some labor laws of Myanmar.

2. Definition of Child in Myanmar

Under the Convention on the Rights of the Child (CRC), "a child means every human being below the age of 18 years unless under the law applicable to the child, majority is attained earlier."[2] However, in Myanmar, there are various definitions and different ranges of age demarcation for defining a child. Under the 1993 Child Law, "child" means a person who has not attained the age of 16 years, and youth means a person at least age 16 but younger than age 18.[3] Some human rights activists criticized that the 1993 Child Law was not consistent with the CRC although the CRC itself includes the clause "unless the law applicable to the child, majority is attained earlier." Under this clause, state parties can stipulate the age of majority according to their national laws.

Section 4(1) of the Guardians and Wards Act provides that a minor is a person who under the provisions of the Majority Act has not attained majority. Under Section 3 of the Majority Act,[4] "a person shall be deemed to have attained his majority when he shall have completed his age of 18 years and not before." According to these two laws,[5] child means a person who has not attained the age of 18 years. Age of majority issues arising from family matters are determined by the respective family law.

Under the 1951 Factories Act, child means a person age at least 14 but not yet 16 who is permitted for employment by a registered practitioner.[6] Adolescent means a person who has attained age 16 years but not age 18.[7]

---

[2] Article 1 of the Convention on the Rights of the Child, 1989.

[3] Section 2(a) and (b) of the Child Law, 1993.

[4] India Act No. IX of 1875.

[5] The Guardians and Wards Act, 1890 and The Majority Act, 1875.

[6] Section 2(a) of the Factories Act, 1951.

[7] Section 2(b), *Ibid.*

According to Sections 2(a) and (b) of the Oil Field (Workers and Welfare) Act, "child means a person who has not attained the age of 15 years and youth means a person who has attained the age of 15 years but has not attained the age of 18 years."

According to the Anti-trafficking in Persons Law, a child is under age 16 and a youth has reached age 16 but not age 18.[8]

Finally, under the Child's Rights Law, child means a person who has not reached age 18.[9] At the present time, irrespective of the laws except the 2019 Child's Rights Law, a person who has attained the age of 18 years becomes the majority in Myanmar.

3. Survival and Development Rights

In Article 6 of the CRC, state parties recognize that every child has the inherent right to life. Regarding these rights, some statutory laws of Myanmar offer the children these survival rights. A child shall enjoy the survival rights before and after birth including citizenship, health, and education.

Under the Child's Rights Law, the state recognizes that every child has the right to survival, development, protection, and care and to participate actively in the community.[10] Under Section 19(a) of said law, "every child has the inherent right to life." Similarly, disabled children enjoy these same fundamental freedoms including the inherent right to life and freedom of speech and religion as well as the rights expressed in the Rights of Persons with Disabilities Law.[11]

As part of protecting the child's rights to the government provides for miscarriage prevention measures. Sections 313 to 318 of the Penal Code provide for imposing punishment to the person who commits the offense of causing miscar-

---

[8] Section 3(j) and (k) of the Anti-trafficking in Persons Law, 2005.

[9] Section 3(b) of the Child's Rights Law, 2019.

[10] Section 18, *Ibid.*

[11] Section 50, *Ibid.*

riage without the woman's consent as well as acts intended to cause miscarriage, to prevent a child's live birth or to cause it to die after birth, or to cause the death of a quick child by an act likely to cause death to a pregnant woman. The law also provides for punishment for exposure and abandonment of children under age 12 by caregivers and for concealing a birth by secret disposal of a dead body. These are the measures that aim to protect an unborn child's right to live.

After a child's birth, the law mandates immediate birth registration. Every child born in the state has the right to free registration of his or her birth without discrimination, and the law imposes on parents, guardians, or any suitable person to inform the relevant government department for birth registration as described.[12] Every child with a registered birth in Myanmar has all rights of citizenship in accordance with the provisions of the existing law,[13] which is stipulated in the constitutions.

According to the constitutions,[14] every person becomes a Myanmar citizen who is born of parents who are both nationals of the Republic of the Union of Myanmar or who are already citizens under the law. Because being a citizen is so important, it is necessary to know the criteria for citizenship. Section 7 of the 1982 Myanmar Citizenship Law describes the citizenship criteria in detail as follows:

"The following persons born in or outside the State are also citizens: -

(a) Persons born of parents, both of whom are citizens;

(b) Persons born of parents, one of whom is a citizen and the other an associate citizen;

(c) Persons born of parents, one of whom and the other a naturalized citizen;

(d) Persons born of parents one of whom is citizen or an associate citizen or a naturalized citizen; and the other is born of parents, both of whom are associate citizens;

---

[12] Section 21(a) and (b), *Ibid.*

[13] Section 22, *Ibid.*

[14] Section 345 of the Constitution of the Republic of the Union of Myanmar, 2008.

(e) Persons born of parents, one of whom is a citizen or an associate citizen or a naturalized citizen; and the other is born of parents, both of whom are a naturalized citizen;

(f) Persons born of parents one of whom is a citizen or an associate citizen or a naturalized citizen; and the other is born of parents, one of whom is an associate citizen and the other is a naturalized citizen."

Therefore, every child shall immediately become a citizen after birth. "Citizenship" is a legal concept describing an individual's relationship to the state. Myanmar's constitution limits that a child can be a citizen only after filling the requirements stipulated in the laws. However, Myanmar never ignores the rights of children who are not citizens. Myanmar obeys all provisions of the CRC. Article 6 of the CRC states that "States Parties shall ensure to the maximum extent possible the survival and development of the child. In order to get survival in live, the child must be healthy and be educated." With regard to health and health services, Article 24 provides in specific detail the right of access to the highest level of health possible and to medical services, with special emphasis on primary and preventive health care, public health education, and decreasing infant mortality.

Similarly, one of the aims of the 2019 Child's Rights Law of Myanmar is to lay down and carry out fundamental measures including health, nutrition, and access to education for children's all-round development.[15] Section 44 of the law grants every child access to health facilities without discrimination and to health care in line with the health policies laid down by the State as well as the right to be able to enjoy physical and mental health in line with health criteria. Toward this goal, every child including newborn children can enjoy all health facilities and measures provided by the Ministry of Health and Sports.[16] Under WHO direction, Myanmar operates its public health services through the relevant ministry. The nation also adopted the Prevention and Control of Communicable Dis-

---

[15] Section 4(c) of the Child's Rights Law, 2019.

[16] Section 45(b), *Ibid.*

ease Law[17] to carry out the child survival measures.

Children's education rights are also important for survival. According to Article 28 of the CRC, every child should have access to the facilities of education provided by the government, and in Myanmar, the Constitution guarantees that every citizen shall have the right to education as compulsory; the state pays special attention to the comprehensive education of its children. Measures in the 2008 Constitution strive earnestly to improve education mandating the provision of free, compulsory primary education under a modern education system[18]; for instance, every citizen has the right to conduct scientific or arts research freely.[19] All citizens irrespective of race, religion, and sex shall be proudly assisted by the Union according to their qualifications,[20] and Section 46 of the 2019 Child's Rights Law provides that "every child shall have the rights to education without discrimination and in line with the National Education Law."[21] In addition, children with disabilities have access to education, including early childhood care and lifelong learning.[22]

Section 47 of the 2019 Child's Rights Law stipulates that the Ministry of Education (MoE) shall focus on providing free basic education in state schools to give children full access to education. The ministry's duty includes establishing any measures necessary for supporting school enrollment and regular school attendance and minimizing untimely drop-out rates. The ministry is also responsible for establishing practical vocational education programs including non-formal education to grant access to children who are unable to attend the state schools.[23]

The specific laws that govern education rights in Myanmar are the National

---

[17] The State Law and Order Restoration Council Law No. 1/1995.

[18] Section 28 of the Constitution of the Republic of the Union of Myanmar, 2008.

[19] Section 366, *Ibid.*

[20] Section 368, *Ibid.*

[21] Section 46(a) and (b) of the Child's Rights Law, 2019.

[22] Section 51(a), *Ibid.*

[23] Section 47, *Ibid.*

Education Law[24] and the Basic Education Law.[25] The MoE is also drafting other specific laws such as the Technical and Vocational Education and Training Law and the Private Education Law. There are not as yet any provisions related to the compulsory free education. The National Education Law (NEL) strengthened the quality, effectiveness, and efficiency of the national education system. The law provides an excellent national framework for implementing a wide range of complementary reforms across the nation, such as recognition of the right of all citizens to free, compulsory education at the primary level; establishment of a standards-based education quality assurance system; expansion of the basic education system to 13 years; support for the learning of nationalities' languages and cultures; and greater decentralization in the education system. An additional benefit of the NEL is that Myanmar is now fully aligned with ASEAN members in terms of the number of years of schooling in basic education.[26] Furthermore, new basic policies in the 2014 NEL include special education programs and services to grant rights to education under the Education for All policy to every school-aged child and youth, including citizens with disability or citizens who have not had a chance to study for whatever reason,[27] as well as implementing the successful free and compulsory education at the primary level and extending step by step.[28]

To implement those policies, the *Pyidaungsu Hluttaw* enacted the Basic Education Law in 2019. Now the MoE has implemented free and compulsory primary education and is striving to extend it to middle school; basic education is to continue for a total of 12 years after kindergarten is completed.[29] The government has increased the education sector's budget allocation in recent years, and this has enabled the MoE to introduce new policies and national programs, such

---

[24] *Pyidaungsu Hluttaw* Law No. 41/2014.

[25] *Pyidaungsu Hluttaw* Law No. 34/2019.

[26] National Education Strategic Plan 2016–21 Summary.

[27] Section 4(c) of the National Education Law, 2014.

[28] Section 4(j), *Ibid.*

[29] Section 5(a) of the Basic Education Law, 2019.

as hiring new teachers, free basic education and the school grants and stipends programs for basic education schools. Furthermore, the department is in the process of drafting the Technical and Vocational Education and Training Law as an effort to reform the technical and vocational education system.

4. Non-Discrimination

Discrimination is the unjustified act of making discriminations between human beings based on the groups, classes, or other categories they are perceived as belonging to. Under the Child's Rights Law,[30] "discrimination is the discriminate treatment on the basis of citizen, tribe, race, cast birth, skin color, sex, language, religion, official position, status, culture, wealth, disability, political belief or sexual orientation." Children should not be discriminated against based on any traits or characteristics; discrimination against children has physical and mental effects on their health that are to be avoided.

Under Article 2.1 of the CRC, all rights apply to all children without exception. It is the obligations of the state to protect children from any form of discrimination based on their or their parents' race, color, sex, language, religion, political or other beliefs or opinions, national, ethnic or social origin, property, disability, birth or other status. Separately under the 2008 Constitution, the Union shall not discriminate against any citizen, based on race, birth, religion, official position, status, culture, sex, or wealth.[31] In short, the law establishes clearly that discrimination is prohibited in Myanmar against any citizen on any basis. However, some human rights activists criticize the word "all citizens," arguing that this stipulation allows for discriminating against noncitizens in Myanmar. However, the Union guarantees any and every person equal rights under the law

---

[30] Section 3(u) of the Child's Rights Law, 2019.
[31] Section 348 of the Constitution of the Republic of the Union of Myanmar, 2008.

and including equal legal protection.[32] Therefore it can be said that there is no discriminatory provision in the 2008 Constitution.

Under Section 4(f) of the Child's Rights Law, all children have equal rights and protections under the existing laws and are not to be discriminated against for any reason.[33] Children born in Myanmar are entitled to freely register their births without discrimination,[34] and the laws hold for health and education rights as well.[35] In addition, under Myanmar Customary Law, there is no discrimination based on gender in adoption and inheritance. Adoption has long been recognized and practiced under Myanmar Customary Law. Any person whether man or woman who is competent to contract can adopt a child, and any adult and any child whether boy or girl can be adopted; in short, adoption is an equal right in Myanmar. Separately, because there is no distinction between male and female for inheritance under Myanmar Customary Law, female children have the right to inherit from either natural or adoptive parents. Therefore, it can be stated that there is no discrimination in Myanmar related to child rights.

5. Best Interests of the Child

"Best interests of the child" is a child rights principle that derives from Article 3 of the CRC: "in all actions regarding children, the best interests of the child must be the first priority to take account into consideration."Therefore, all actions concerning children such as all custody discussions and decisions are made with the ultimate goal of fostering and encouraging the child's happiness, security, mental health, and emotional development into young adulthood. In addition, public or private social welfare institutions, courts of law, administrative authorities, and legislative bodies shall consider primarily this principle in their action

---

[32] Section 347, *Ibid.*

[33] Section 19(d) of the Child's Rights Law, 2019.

[34] Section 21(a), *Ibid.*

[35] Sections 44(a) and 46(a), *Ibid.*

concerning children. Accordingly, Myanmar considers the best interests of the child the highest priority, and the Child's Rights Law reflects this principle. One of the purposes of this legislation is to promote the child's best interests.[36]

The best interests of the child mean the child's rights and access to the greatest physical and mental benefits as provided under the 2008 Constitution and the Child's Rights Law to enjoy their survival, development, protection, and right to participate in society.[37] Under Section 19(b) of this law, meeting the child's interests includes in cases of child care, disabilities, juvenile justice, and adoption, and Article 21 of the CRC also recognizes inter-country adoption as an alternative for ensuring that the child's best interests are being met.

In Myanmar, adoption is governed under Sections 25 to 32 of the Child's Rights Law. A Myanmar citizen has the right to adopt a child in accordance with the stipulations of law if he can treat and nurture the child as the child's natural parents would.[38] Under this section, only Myanmar citizens can adopt, and this prohibition against foreign adoption is the state's effort to avoid sanctioning or supporting child-related offenses such as human sale or trafficking or abduction to a foreign country. Persons in Myanmar who want to adopt can do so by registering an adoption deed in either the social welfare office or the relevant registration office in accordance with the Registration of *Kittima* Adoption Act of 1939.[39] Under this Act, adopted children are protected against such offenses as smuggling, sale, forced labor, and torture committed by or in collaboration with the adoptive parents.[40] Adopted children also have the right to inherit ancestral property of adoptive parents and other rights.[41]

At present, Rules 61, 62, and 63 of the Rules Relating to Child Law, 1993 (although the 1993 Child Law has already been repealed, the new rules have not yet

---

[36] Section 4(b), *Ibid.*

[37] Section 3(d), *Ibid.*

[38] Section 25, *Ibid.*

[39] Section 27(b), *Ibid.*

[40] Section 29(c), *Ibid.*

[41] Section 32(b), *Ibid.*

been enacted) are the provisions for adoption procedures. Adoption in Myanmar is related to not only parental but also property rights, and toward the latter goal, the Registration of *Kittima* Adoption Act is an existing provision for strong legal protections of a child's inheritance rights.

The best interests of the child must also be taken into account in caring for children.[42] If parents are separated, either or both must still consider the child's best interests in the child's upbringing.[43] Child Rights Law Section 38(b) stipulates that a person who wants to take care of a child can apply to the court for a guardianship decree, but the person must want the best interests of the child. The relevant court is responsible for appointing said guardian, whether a parent, grandparent, or blood relative, considering the child's best interests based on age and maturity.[44]

In terms of legal matters and juvenile justice, the Juvenile Court in Myanmar has duties in consideration of a child offender's best interests. Specifically, the courts have the duty to consider the child's age and character as well as environmental circumstances, the reason for committing the offense, and any probation officer report as well as other matters, and the courts are mandated to prioritize the process of child custody and diversion, if possible, without compromising the child's freedom.[45]

Myanmar Customary Law also adjudicates some matters related to a child's best interests. Family separations incur child custody issues. According to the *Dhammathats*,[46] if the divorce is by mutual consent, the husband is entitled to the custody of the sons and the wife to that of the daughters except that very young sons should remain with their mothers until they are more mature. However, parents do have the discretion to make their own custody arrangements irrespective

---

[42] Section 34, *Ibid.*

[43] Section 36(b) *Ibid.*

[44] Sections 39(a) and (b), *Ibid.*

[45] Section 87, *Ibid.*

[46] U Gaung, *A Digest of the Burmese Buddhist Law Concerning Inheritance and Marriage*, Volume II, Marriage, Section 234.

of the *Dhammathats* with the stipulation that courts will not support a parent's rights against the child's interests or welfare. When children are old enough to make a rational determination, their wishes are paramount.[47] In the case of a divorce by matrimonial fault, *Dhammathats* do not clearly say which parent has the right to custody of the children; questions relating to divorce and child custody are the concern of solely the Guardians and Wards Act of 1890 with the focus as ever on the best interest of the child.

6. Protection

Children have the right to be protected from physical and mental violence, neglect, sexual abuse and exploitation while they are in the custody of their parents or any other person. Article 3.2 of the CRC ensures children the right to this protection, and Article 19 makes it a state's responsibility to protect children from all forms of maltreatment by responsible others including undertaking prevention and treatment programs in this regard. Children without families are protected by the Social Welfare Department; the Ministry of Social Welfare, Relief and Resettlement; and some religious organizations.

Myanmar protects children from economic exploitation and from performing any work that is likely to be hazardous or to interfere with the child's education, or to be harmful to the child's health or physical, mental, spiritual, moral or social development in line with Article 32 of the CRC. Myanmar also ratified the Optional Protocol to the Convention on the Rights of the Child on the Sale of Children, Child Prostitution and Child Pornography and the Optional Protocol, which followed the enactment of the new Child Rights Law in July 2019. That law defines the terms "sale of children, child prostitution, child pornography, and exploitation" in accordance with "the optional protocol."[48] The 1993 Child Law

---

[47] Po Cho v. Ma Nyein Myat, 5 L.B.R. 133.

[48] The Optional Protocol to the Convention on the Rights of the Child on the Sale of Chil-

did not provide these definitions.

Protecting children in the criminal justice system is governed under both the Penal Code and the Child's Rights Law. Under Section 82 of the Penal Code, a child under seven years of age is absolutely exempted from criminal liability, and under Section 83, a child above seven and under twelve years of age is exempted from imposed punishment if he or she lacks the maturity to understand the nature and consequence of the offending conduct. Somewhat differently, under the Child's Rights Law, children under age 10 years can be entirely exempted from criminal liability, as can children over age 10 and under age 12, if they do not understand the consequences of their acts.[49] Briefly, children under age 10 in Myanmar are legally innocent and cannot be convicted of or punished for any crimes, and the same can apply to children over 10 but under 12 under certain circumstances. Therefore, it is necessary to amend the Penal Code to bring it in alignment with the Child's Rights Law.

Before Myanmar joined the CRC, the Penal Code protected the nation's minors. Under the Penal Code, kidnapping was punishable by imprisonment for up to seven years and could incur a fine as well.[50] Procuring minor children for sale or purchase for the purpose of prostitution[51] was punishable with imprisonment up to ten years and potentially a fine. Rape against a girl under age 12 was punishable for at least 20 years and up to life.[52] After Myanmar joined the CRC, the nation passed a specific law for children, namely, the 1993 Child Law. Under the 1993 Child Law, the above offenses are punishable with imprisonment up to two years, a fine of up to 10,000 kyats, or both.[53] Although this law clearly imposes fines, it is overall more lenient than the Penal Code, and it was repealed by the 2019 Child's Rights Law.

---

dren, Child Prostitution and Child Pornography, 2000.

[49] Section 78 of the Child's Rights Law, 2019.

[50] Section 363 of the Penal Code, 1861.

[51] Sections 366 A, 372, and 373, *Ibid.*

[52] Section 376(c), *Ibid.*

[53] Section 66 of the Child Law, 1993.

Under the 2019 law, it is prohibited to commit physical, mental, or sexual violence against a child,[54] even during armed conflict, and children are also protected from neglect and exploitation.[55] The 2019 Child's Rights Law also prohibits any sexual exploitation, forced sex work, or child pornography and imposes specific penalties on perpetrators of such crimes.[56] Other punishable crimes include mental and physical violence such as spanking, and this offense is punishable with one to six months in prison, a fine of 100,000 to 300,000 kyats, or both.[57] It is also prohibited to allow children to work in any clubs, karaoke bars, or massage parlors; this crime is punishable with imprisonment for five months up to two years, a fine of between 500,000 and 1,000,000 kyats, or both.[58]

Other violations of a child's rights include forcing a child to beg, which punishes the accused with imprisonment of six months to three years, a fine of 600,000 to 1,200,000 kyats, or both,[59] as well as the following: committing offenses of violence, abuse, exploitation, or discrimination against children with disabilities; employing children in work that causes physical, emotional, or reputational harm; or torture, cruelty, inhuman or degrading treatment. These crimes are punishable with imprisonment of eight months to maximum of five years or a fine of 800,000 to 1,600,000 kyats.[60] Committing physical or mental violence against a child during armed conflict shall be punished with imprisonment for one to six years and a fine of 900,000 to 1,800,000 kyats.[61]

Further protections for children under the 2019 Child's Rights Law include prohibitions against forced marriage and against knowingly allowing a child under one's guardianship to live with a prostitute or work as a prostitute. These

---

[54] Section 56 of the Child's Rights Law, 2019.

[55] Section 62(a), *Ibid.*

[56] Section 66, *Ibid.*

[57] Section 100(a), *Ibid.*

[58] Section 101(b), *Ibid.*

[59] Section 102, *Ibid.*

[60] Section 103(a), *Ibid.*

[61] Section 103(b), *Ibid.*

crimes are punishable with prison terms of one to seven years and fines between 1,000,000 and 2,000,000 kyats.[62] Crimes of employing children as prostitutes and attempting to exchange money to abduct or sexually exploit a child is punishable with imprisonment for a minimum of two and a maximum of ten years and a fine of a minimum of 1,200,000 and a maximum of 1,500,000 kyats.[63] Finally, any offense related to selling, purchasing, or illegally removing, transferring, or knowingly replacing a child's internal organs incurs a penalty of imprisonment between 10 and 20 years and a fine between 50,000,000 and 100,000,000 kyats.[64] In short, the 2019 Child's Rights Law provides for more severe punishments than either 1993 law or the Penal Code, and Myanmar protects children from all forms of sexual exploitation and sexual abuse.

Exploitation of children can also take place in the context of drug use. Under Section 22(c) of the 1993 Narcotic Drugs and Psychotropic Substances Law, using children under age 16 to commit offenses provided in Sections 16 to 21 of the law is punishable by the maximum penalty allowed under the law. This law protects children exploitation in drug smuggling. However, since the enactment of the Child's Rights Law, child-related drug smuggling offenses are now only punishable under that law.[65]

Moreover, the Civil Procedure Code of 1909 provides for some legal actions involving children, for instance the right to sue and be sued through the next friend for the minor plaintiff and the guardian for the minor defendant.[66] Such next friend or guardian for the suit is prohibited from entering into, without the expressly recorded leave of the Court, any agreement or compromise on behalf of the minor in the suit. Such agreements are voidable against all parties other than the minor.[67] Therefore, it is clear that Myanmar always considered children's best

---

[62] Section 105(a), *Ibid.*

[63] Section 105(b), *Ibid.*

[64] Section 106, *Ibid.*

[65] Section 119, *Ibid.*

[66] Rule 1 of Order XXXII of the Civil Procedure Code, 1909.

[67] Rule 7, *Ibid.*

interests under the Penal Code and the Civil Procedure Code before the country passed the Child' Rights Law, 2019.

The Republic of the Union of Myanmar prohibits human enslaving and trafficking and forced labor,[68] and the laws discussed above indicate that no one including children is allowed to commit human trafficking or forced labor. Moreover, mothers and children as well as expectant women including fallen soldiers' families enjoy equal rights as prescribed by law.[69] Meanwhile, the Ministry of Labor, Immigration and Population protects children with regard to workplace safety and prevention of infringement and loss of their rights.[70] Other laws on children's rights to work are the 1951 Factories Act, the 1951 Oil Field (Workers of Welfare) Act, the 2016 Shops and Establishments Law, and the 2019 Child's Rights Law.

The 1951 Factories Act prohibited employing any child under age 14 to work in any factory.[71] The 1951 Oil Field Act sets 13 as the minimum employment age[72]; additionally, children over 13 without a medical fitness certificate are also prohibited from working in an oil field.[73] A medical practitioner can certify a child over 15 years as fit to work as an adult,[74] so this Act needs to be amended to prohibit children under 14 years from working in oil fields. Children over age 15 should also be prohibited from this hazardous work.

The Shops and Establishments Law, 2016, prohibits children under the age of 14 to be employed in shops and establishments,[75] in line with the International Labor Standards. This Act allows the children between 14 and 16 to work if certified by a registered medical practitioner.[76] Under the Child's Rights Law, 2019,

---

[68] Sections 358 and 359 of the Constitution of the Republic of the Union of Myanmar, 2008.

[69] Sections 32(a) and 351, *Ibid.*

[70] Section 24 of the Child's Rights Law, 2019.

[71] Section 75 of the Factories Act, 1951.

[72] Section 52 of the Oil Field (Workers of Welfare) Act, 1951.

[73] Section 53, *Ibid.*

[74] Section 54(2) (b), *Ibid.*

[75] Section 13(a) of the Shops and Establishments Law, 2016.

[76] Section 14(a), *Ibid.*

14 is the age for a child to work unless the stipulated age for free and compulsory basic education is over the age of 14. Children over the stipulated age who are in good health and able to work can engage in work in accordance with the labor laws.[77] It can be seen that the age limit for a child to work differs across different laws, and these require uniformity as well as alignment with international standards.

With regards to the working hours, no child shall be employed or permitted to work in any factory for more than four hours in any day.[78] With respect to the working hours for young workers aged between 16 and 18 years, those who have been granted a fit certificate to work as adults can work the same working hours as adults.[79] Otherwise, those young workers who have not been granted a fit certificate are governed under Section 79(1) (a) of this law, which sets four hours as the young workers' maximum. International Labor Standards allows same working hours as adults for young workers beyond 15 years. Therefore, it should be amended to align with the International Labor Standards.

However, the 2016 Shops and Establishments Law stipulates that a person who has not attained the age of 16 years shall not be allowed to work overtime more than prescribed working hours in any shop or establishment.[80] Moreover, children between 14 and 16 years with a fit certificate for work cannot be allowed to work for more than four hours a day.[81] Young workers over 16 years are allowed the same working hours as adults. This is in line with the International Labor Standards stipulated for young workers over 15 years, but the Act allows overtime and night work for young workers over 16 years, and therefore it should be amended.

Myanmar signed ILO Convention No. 182, Worst Forms of Child Labor Convention, 1999 in 2013. Therefore, the forms of child labor mentioned in the Sec-

---

[77] Section 48, of the Child's Rights Law, 2019.
[78] Section 79(1) (a) of the Factories Act, 1951.
[79] Section 78(1), *Ibid.*
[80] Section 13(b) of the Shops and Establishments Law, 2016.
[81] Section 14(a), *Ibid.*

tion 2(t) of the 2019 Child's Rights Law protect the child from being employed in the worst forms. The child shall be prevented from engaging in the worst forms of child labor.[82]

The ILO Convention No. 6 on Night Work of Young Persons (Industry), 1919, was ratified by Myanmar in 1921. Article 2(1) of that Convention No. 6 prohibits employment of children under the age of 18 years to night work.

In Myanmar, the children are prohibited to employ or permit to work at night in any factory.[83] Moreover, any youth who has not got fit certificate for employment by a registered medical practitioner shall not be employed or allowed to employ at a factory at night.[84]

But, according to the Shops and Establishments Law, 2016, any person who has attained the age of 14 years, but not 16 years shall not be compelled or allowed to work at night.[85] Therefore, it is necessary to amend these provisions in line with the Convention No. 6.

Children under 18 years old are forbidden from doing dangerous, unhealthy work that is bad for their morals and physical situations. The government, therefore, needs to make a list of hazardous work that a child should not be doing under 18 years.[86]

In Myanmar, it is provided in the Child's Rights Law that the Ministry of Labor, Immigration, and Population shall specify the types of hazardous works and workplaces in consultation with the organizations of employers and the relevant trade unions.[87] However, the ministry has not provided any such list of hazardous works, and there are no provisions in the 1951 Factories Act and the 2016 Shops and Establishments Law.

In the 1951 Factories Act, no young person shall work or be required to work

---

[82] Section 48(a) of the Child's Rights Law, 2019.

[83] Section 79(1)(b) of the Factories Act, 1951.

[84] Section 78(3), *Ibid.*

[85] Section 14(b) of the Shops and Establishments Law, 2016.

[86] Article 3 of the ILO Convention No. 138 and Article 4 of the ILO Convention No. 182.

[87] Section 49(a) of the Child's Rights Law, 2019.

at any machine unless he has been fully instructed as to the dangers arising in connection there with and the precautions to be taken.[88] Moreover, no woman or child shall be employed in any part of a factory in which a cotton opener is at work.[89] Then, no youth shall be instructed to work by means that cause danger, health impacts, hindrance the right to education, hurt to the character and dignity.[90] Young workers under 18 years are prohibited from working in dangerous work.[91] If any child has been forced to work in a hazardous workplace, the employer shall be punished as mentioned in the Child's Rights Law.[92] Therefore, the provisions for the protection of children should be updated in line with the current Child's Rights Law and the International Labor Standards.

The 2005 Anti-Trafficking in Persons Law declares that it is a "national duty" "to prevent and suppress the trafficking in persons as it damages the pride and pedigree of Myanmar nationality that should be valued and safeguarded by the Myanmar race".[93] The law further pays particular attention to women, children, and youth for preventing and suppressing trafficking in persons.[94] Under this law, persons who traffic women and children shall be punished with serious imprisonment.[95] This law is certainly welcoming and commendable in light of the high incidences of human trafficking. Nonetheless, in order to effectively eliminate child trafficking, some improvements should be made.

---

[88] Section 25(1) of the Factories Act, 1951.

[89] Section 29, *Ibid.*

[90] Section 75 A, *Ibid.*

[91] Section 14(d) of the Shops and Establishments Law, 2016.

[92] Section 103(a) (2) and (3) of the Child's Rights Law, 2019.

[93] Section 4(a) of the Anti-trafficking in Persons Law, 2005.

[94] Section 4(b), *Ibid.*

[95] Section 24, *Ibid.*

7. Conclusion

Children are regarded as "jewels" of the society. Promulgation of the Child Law in 1993 (this law has been already repealed) two years after Myanmar's accession to the Convention on the Rights of the Child in 1991 and subsequent adoption of the Rules of the Child Law are significant achievements in promoting and protecting the rights of the children in Myanmar. Then, in 2019, the State newly enacted the Child's Rights Law to define a child as anyone under the age of 18. Today, all children born in Myanmar are guaranteed the fundamental and unconditional right to register at birth. Birth registration is the first right of the child and a stepping stone to enjoying other rights such as the right to health, education and protection. With the establishment of a minimum age for marriage (18 years) and for employment (14 years), the value of childhood is recognized and helps allow children to be children. The law also recognizes that children affected by armed conflict need special protection by criminalizing grave violations against children and providing stronger legal protection for children in the context of armed conflict.

We are today trying our utmost to create better opportunities for the children so that they can live in a better world enjoying the full range of their rights. Today's enactment of the Child's Rights Law demonstrates Myanmar's commendable efforts to align national policies and regulatory frameworks with the UN Convention on the Rights of the Child. Therefore, children in Myanmar have got the rights and protection especially given by Child's Rights Law, 2019 including the constitution and other statutory laws.

Chapter 7

GLOBALIZATION IMPACT ON THE RULE OF LAW:

International Trade Law and Domestic Law Reform

Dao Gia Phuc*

(The University of Economics and Law)

1. Economic Globalization and the Rule of Law

In recent decades, the term "economic globalization" has been widely used by politicians, businesspeople, environmentalists, economists, and lawyers; it describes one of the defining features of the world we live in today. Joseph Stiglitz, former Chief Economist of the World Bank and winner of the Nobel Prize for Economics in 2001, described the concept as follows:

The closer integration of the countries and people of the world which has been brought about by the enormous reduction of costs of transportation and communication, and the breaking down of artificial barriers to the flow of goods, services, capita, knowledge, and (to the lesser extent) people across borders.[1]

---

* Vice-Director of the American Law Center, The University of Economics and Law, Viet Nam National University in Ho Chi Minh city.
[1] Joseph Stiglitz, *Globalization and Its Discontents* (Penguin UK, 2015), 9.

Thomas Friedman, the award-winning journalist of the New York Times, also defined globalization as follows:

It is the inexorable integration of markets, nation-states, and technologies to a degree never witnessed before – in a way that is enabling individuals, corporations, and nation-states farther, faster, deeper, and cheaper than ever before.[2]

Bossche and Zdouc expanded on the concept to state that economic globalization is the gradual integration of national economies into one borderless global economy by compassing (free) international trade and (unrestricted) foreign direct investment (FDI).[3] Thus, it affects people everywhere in all aspects of their daily lives, such as jobs, health, education, and even leisure time. Technology and trade liberalization have been recognized as main drivers of economic globalization.[4] The former has erased the natural barriers of time and space that hindered national economies have faded through advances in computing and communications, the latter makes these changes happen. Today, businesses are even able to fragment production across continents, thanks to technological innovation and the emergence of a rules-based trading environment.

Indisputably, in the past 30 years, many countries have experienced rapid growth in foreign trade, FDI, and inflows and outflows of foreign capital.[5] The accession in domestic markets by multinational corporations and the increased cross-border movement of technology, information, capital, and management skills have altered the domestic production patterns in many states. By acceding to various treaties and joining international organizations such as the World

---

[2] Thomas L. Friedman, *The Lexus and the Olive Tree* (HarperCollins, 2000), 9.

[3] Peter Van den Bossche and Werner Zdouc, *The Law and Policy of the World Trade Organization: Text, Cases and Materials* (Cambridge University Press, 2017), 4.

[4] Martin Wolf, "Globalisation," *Financial Times*, June 13, 2013.

[5] Robert Wade, "Globalization and Its Limits: Reports of the Death of the National Economy Are Greatly Exaggerated," *National Diversity and Global Capitalism* 8 (1996): 62–64.

Trade Organization (WTO), states have created a supranational legal order that threatens their sovereignty. In the more radical view, some commentators believe that the nation-state as an economic unit has ended and the birth of a borderless world has just begun.[6]

There has been a notable rise in anti-globalization and anti-trade rhetoric by populists in many countries owing to widespread concern about the harmful effects of economic globalization and international trade, including jobs and wages, global ecosystems, economic development, cultural identity and diversity, and national sovereignty. However, the figures have shown that international trade is a vital generator for reducing poverty.[7] Specifically, the countries with intensified links with the global economy through trade have proliferated over a sustained period and have experienced more significant poverty declines. Although at low levels, globalization does often appear to hurt the poor, beyond a certain threshold it in fact reduces poverty.[8] Therefore, trade liberalization is one of the few policies that virtually all economists can agree on.

Likewise, FDI is arguably even more critical as an engine of global economic integration. Businesses build plants, bring in machinery, and supply technology, which all create jobs. Although some potential issues are inherent, an OECD study showed that the benefits of FDI generally greatly outweigh the costs.[9] Said benefits to host countries include not only jobs, tax revenues, and economic growth but also "spill over benefits" such as improving the quality of the local labor force and improving management skills, as well as the introduction of new technology and the transfer of technical know-how.[10] The study findings dispute

---

[6] See generally Arthur Selwyn Miller, "The Global Corporation and American Constitutionalism: Some Political Consequences of Economic Power," *J. Int'l L. & Econ.* 6 (1971): 235; Kenichi Ohmae, "The Borderless World.," *McKinsey Quarterly*, no. 3 (1990): 3–19; and Susan Strange and Scholar of International Relations Susan Strange, *The Retreat of the State: The Diffusion of Power in the World Economy* (Cambridge University Press, 1996).

[7] See Pierre-Richard Agénor, *Does Globalization Hurt the Poor?* (The World Bank, 2002).

[8] Ibid.

[9] OECD, *Foreign Direct Investment for Development*, 2002.

[10] Ibid.

the anti-globalization claim that multinational corporations move production to developing countries to avoid stringent labor and environmental standards. In the OECD study, foreign-owned enterprises operating in developing countries typically paid higher wages and followed higher environmental standards when they invested.[11] The report concedes that FDI can result in some unintended side effects, including competition with local firms, job losses at those firms, and volatility in the balance of payments related to major investors' import and export activities. However, the report also notes that such problems are generally temporary and can be mitigated by appropriate host country policies.[12]

However, it is noteworthy that all these engines of economic development depend on the rule of law. In defining this term, scholars and practitioners often refer to Fuller's list of the virtues inherent in an actual system of law: (1) the law is general in its application; (2) the law is public; (3) the law operates prospectively; (4) the law is reasonably clear; (5) the law is internally consistent; (6) the law is practicable to comply with; (7) the law is relatively stable; and (8) there is a congruence between the letter of the law and how it is enforced.[13] These eight criteria specify necessary conditions for law-making, which is "the enterprise of subjecting human conduct to the governance of rules."[14] Raz borrows from Fuller's formal components to include principles of institutional design, namely the guaranteed independence of the judiciary and the principles of natural justice, judicial review, and access to justice.[15] Tamanaha also states that the rule of law exists, in its most basic terms, when government officials and citizens are generally bound by and abide by the law.[16] Through this lens, the fundamental, instru-

---

[11] Ibid.

[12] Ibid.

[13] Lon L. Fuller, *The Morality of Law* (New Haven, Conn.: Yale Univ. Press, 1964), 39.

[14] Ibid. at 106.

[15] Joseph Raz, "The Rule of Law and Its Virtue, The Authority of Law: Essays on Law and Morality," *Oxford: Oxford University Press* 210 (1979): 214–18.

[16] Brian Z. Tamanaha, "The Primacy of Society and the Failures of Law and Development," *Cornell Int'l LJ* 44 (2011): 9.

mental virtue of a legal system is, therefore, manifest as the rule of law.

In today's complex world, the rule of law is more critical to those ends. The flows of capital, international trade, and foreign investment require legal certainty and transparency, and these requirements are demanding in many developing countries.[17] Carothers identifies three types of rule of law reform undertaken in countries transitioning to democracy, distinguishing among them based on the extend of reform.[18] Type one reform focuses on rewriting laws, mainly commercial and criminal. Type two reform involves strengthening law-related institutions through increasing salaries for judges and court staff; training police, prosecutors, public defenders, and correctional officers; and improving legal education and local government legislatures. Type three reform focuses on the government's compliance with the law – the type of reform most needed in emerging democracies around the world. As Carothers notes, rewriting constitutions, laws, and regulations is comparatively easy against the burden of institutional reform because much of the impetus must come from inside government.[19]

Unfortunately, many studies have shown that such institutions might be difficult to change.[20] Moreover, it is unclear that these institutions are responsive to change from external forces. One problem is that these institutions are intimately linked to particular distributive outcomes, and therefore, attempts to change them may run into significant political opposition, as Srinivasan argues.[21] However, other researchers have been more optimistic in highlighting that several de-

---

[17] Delissa A. Ridgway and Mariya A. Talib, "Globalization and Development - Free Trade, Foreign Aid, Investment and the Rule of Law Essay," *Cal. W. Int'l L.J.* 33, no. 2 (2002–2003): 337.

[18] Thomas Carothers, "The Rule of Law Revival," *Foreign Aff.* 77 (1998): 95.

[19] Ibid.

[20] Kevin E. Davis and Michael J. Trebilcock, "The Relationship between Law and Development: Optimists versus Skeptics," *The American Journal of Comparative Law* 56, no. 4 (2008): 895–946.

[21] Thirukodikaval N. Srinivasan and Jessica Seddon Wallack, "Globalization, Growth, and the Poor," *De Economist* 152, no. 2 (2004): 251–272.

veloping countries have achieved high growth rates over long periods by adopting good policies and sound governance. Braithwaite clarifies that developing countries can sometimes benefit from institutional links formed by developed countries in an interconnected world.[22] Barr also argues that positive institutional growth can occur in developing countries despite governmental frameworks' weakness.[23]

From the perspective of international law, international trade and investment treaties complement the pursuit of humanitarian and other normative ends, which contributes to sustainable development. The 164 Member States to the Marrakesh Agreement (1994), the founding document for the WTO, agreed in principle to make

optimal use of the world's resources in accordance with the objective of sustainable development, seeking both to protect and preserve the environment and to enhance the means for doing so in a manner consistent with their respective needs and concerns at different levels of economic development.[24]

While the language used does not impose binding obligations on WTO members, the agreement implies an obligation to work in good faith toward integrating and accommodating sustainable development principles in international trade and investment practices. International treaties like the Convention on the Illegal Trade in Endangered Species and national custom and environmental laws prohibiting the importation of illegally sourced forest and marine resources demonstrate states' interest in preventing environmental destruction, further constraining the scope for transnational organized crime. Even though countries

---

[22] John Braithwaite, *Regulatory Capitalism: How It Works, Ideas for Making It Work Better* (Edward Elgar Publishing, 2008).

[23] Michael S. Barr and Geoffrey P. Miller, "Global Administrative Law: The View from Basel," *European Journal of International Law* 17, no. 1 (2006): 15–46.

[24] Marrakesh agreement (also Agreement establishing the World Trade Organization) (1994). https://www. wto.org/english/docs_e/legal_e/04-wto.pdf. Accessed 14 November 2020.

that depend on timber and fisheries exports are concerned that the documentation levels necessary to satisfy legal requirements stretch the limits of their regulatory and law enforcement capacities, such prohibitions do not constitute a restraint of trade under WTO rules.[25] Though we might expect all humanitarian, human rights, and sustainability norms to run second to state and private commercial priorities, these are not incompatible ends.[26]

2. The Proliferation of Regional Trade Agreements and the Rule of Law

The history of regionalism can be observed in many parts of the world. Regional economic integration first became an essential focus in Europe in the 1950s and 1960s, mainly intending to build peace after World War II through the establishment of the European Economic Community in 1958. In Latin America, efforts at economic cooperation focused on promoting industrialization by substituting imports from the US with regional production. In Africa, the establishment of regional institutions, such as African Unity in 1963 (nowadays the African Union), was concurrent with the increase of independent states. In Asia, the Association of Southeast Asian Nations found their association in 1967 (ASEAN).[27]

Traditionally, regional economic integration was negotiated to address needs

---

[25] See generally Paul Battersby, *The Unlawful Society: Global Crime and Security in a Complex World* (Springer, 2014).

[26] See Diane A. Desierto, "The International Mandate for Development: Building Compliant Investment within the State's Development Decision-Making Processes," in *International Investment Law and Development* (Edward Elgar Publishing, 2015), 333–68; and Valentina Sara Vadi, "Access to Medicines versus Protection of 'Investments' in Intellectual Property: Reconciliation through Interpretation?," *Law in the Pursuit of Development: Principles into Practice?*, 2009, 52–67.

[27] Theresa Carpenter, "A Historical Perspective on Regionalism," in *Multilateralizing Regionalism: Challenges for the Global Trading System*, ed. Richard Baldwin and Patrick Low (Cambridge University Press, 2009), 13–27.

for cooperation beyond the nation-state that could form the basis for a more profound political coalition.[28] More recently, regional arrangements on trade developed with other aims beyond geographic proximity. This trend can been referred to as the "new regionalism," which accepts that groups can be defined by features other than geographic location such as cultural, linguistic, social or historical bonds.[29] Thus, governments today recognize regional trade agreements (RTAs) by the mutual interests of parties rather than the geography.

This new regional approach to trade cooperation featured deeper economic integration with the formation of the European Union (EU), the North American Free Trade Agreement, and MERCOSUR (Southern Common Market-Mercado Común del Sur).[30] Inspired by the establishment of these trade blocs in the Americas and Europe in the late 1980s and early 1990s, the number of RTAs has flourished in the last two decades.[31] The reasons for this proliferation of RTAs originated from the difficulties confronted in the Uruguay Round, which motivated several countries to pursue preferential deals as an alternative in case multilateral trade negotiations with the WTO failed.[32] Additionally, over the past 50

---

[28] David Mitrany, "A Working Peace System," in *The European Union* (Palgrave, London, 1994), 77–97; and Ernst B Haas, *Beyond the Nation State: Functionalism and International Organization* (ECPR Press, 2008); and Ernst B. Haas and Desmond Dinan, *The Uniting of Europe: Political, Social, and Economic Forces, 1950–1957*, vol. 311 (Stanford University Press Stanford, 1958).

[29] For instance, under the WTO definition of RTAs, an agreement between the United States and Jordan is considered "regional." See Tanja A. Börzel and Thomas Risse, "Introduction: Framework of the Handbook and Conceptual Clarifications," in *The Oxford Handbook of Comparative Regionalism*, ed. Tanja Börzel and Thomas Risse (Oxford University Press, 2016), 3–15.

[30] Louise Fawcett, "Exploring Regional Domains: A Comparative History of Regionalism," *International Affairs* 80, no. 3 (2004): 440; Fredrik Söderbaum, "Early, Old, New and Comparative Regionalism: The Scholarly Development of the Field," 2015, 18.

[31] By December 2018, the WTO had received 681 notifications of RTAs, 467 of which were in force at that time. See https://www.wto.org/english/tratop_e/region_e/region_e.htm#facts, accessed on 11 May 2019.

[32] For instance, the expansion of the European RTAs network included countries from Central and Eastern Europe, the Balkans, and the Mediterranean; the influence from the U.S for

years, the number of WTO Member States grew to 164 as of 2019, and this broad membership might have caused an impasse in multilateral trade liberalization. Such difficulties were revealed in the collapse of the trade deal during the 2013 WTO Ministerial Conference in the Doha Round.[33] Therefore, WTO members have considered RTAs possible alternatives for improving economic welfare and domestic industries' profits.[34]

In actuality, the WTO with its 164 member countries is the only international trade organization; it provides the necessary legal infrastructure of trade and a mechanism for enforcement. The RTAs, meanwhile, could provide new rules that the WTO has failed to create and those that could elaborate and refine the organization's rules. In this regard, the WTO and RTAs complement to each other, and the combination of rules between them can help international trade regime be more transparent and comprehensive. Specifically, RTAs would support deeper commitments than the ones typically granted at the multilateral level, moving forward a trade agenda among a small group of countries.

Consequently, RTAs could experiment as laboratories for new and sensitive trade-related issues.[35] Moreover, RTAs may cover not only trade matters in a narrow sense, but also other issues that cannot be settled at a multilateral level such as labor, environmental and competition standards.[36] Once an RTA is con-

---

a strong preference towards preferential agreements; the regionalism-oriented policies from Chile, Mexico, and Singapore aim to establish preferential relations with their major trading partners; the fragmentation of the former Soviet Union states looked for new trade organizations. See Rafael Leal-Arcas, "Proliferation of Regional Trade Agreements: Complementing or Supplanting Multilateralism," *Chi. J. Int'l L.* 11 (2010–2011): 597–630.

[33] Doha Round is the most recent round of trade negotiations within WTO. It was launched in November 2011. See https://www.wto.org/english/tratop_e/dda_e/dda_e.htm. Accessed July, 29th.

[34] Scott L. Baier et al., "Do Economic Integration Agreements Actually Work? Issues in Understanding the Causes and Consequences of the Growth of Regionalism," *World Economy* 31, no. 4 (2008): 465.

[35] Richard E Baldwin, "Multilateralising Regionalism: Spaghetti Bowls as Building Blocs on the Path to Global Free Trade," *World Economy* 29, no. 11 (2006): 1451–1518.

[36] E. K. Kessie, "The World Trade Organization and Regional Trade Agreements : An Analy-

cluded among a small number of WTO members, other members may follow this approach and multilateralize the idea. Practically, many WTO members started to negotiate several sensitive trade-related issues at the bilateral or at regional level and only then brought to the multilateral negotiations in the WTO.[37] Ironically, several developed countries such as the US and EU, nowadays, substituted its multilateralism strategy with an ambitious bilateral and plurilateral trade liberalization agenda, aimed at removing the behind-the-border barriers to trade through regulating "deep" disciplines, including public procurement, intellectual property rights protection.[38] Notably, in along and largely in synergy with "deep" disciplines, the "new generation" or "21st century" RTAs have been marked by the proliferation of non-trade-related measures, such as sustainable development and human rights.[39] For example, the two critical developments mark the EU's contemporary development agenda concerning trade liberalization and the rule of law. The first one deals with a growing recognition of the role that laws and their observance play in promoting sustainable development in general and its selected aspects, such as sustainable trade.[40] On the other hand, trade liberalization is often increasingly viewed as a means to foster fundamental values, including the rule of law, in third countries.[41]

---

sis of the Relevant Rules of the WTO," Sydney (Thesis, The University of Technology, Doctor of Juridical Science, 2001), 31–55.

[37] Joy A. Kim, "Harnessing Regional Trade Agreements for the Post-2012 Climate Change Regime," *Climate and Trade*, 2009, 57.

[38] For the EU's alteration to the bilateral and plurilateral trade agenda, see: European Commission, Communication to the Council, the European Economic and Social Committee and the Committee of the Regions "Global Europe: Competing in the World," COM (2006) 567 final of 4 October 2006.

[39] For the concept of the EU's "new generation" of RTAs, see: European Commission DG "Trade" (2016) Strategic Plan 2016–2020. https://trade.ec.europa.eu/doclib/docs/2016/august/tradoc_154919.pdf.

[40] See Maryna Rabinovych, "Where Economic Development Meets the Rule of Law? Promoting Sustainable Development Goals Through the European Neighborhood Policy," *Brill Open Law* 2, no. 1 (April 3, 2020): 140–74.

[41] Axel Marx et al., "Global Governance through Trade: An Introduction," *Elgar Online: The*

A typical new-generation RTAs with non-traded-related measures concerning the rule of law entails two elements. Firstly, it contains a clause specifying the core values "underpinning the relationships between the Parties" (a substantive "essential element" clause).[42] Secondly, a "suspension clause" defines the procedure for suspending an agreement or parts thereof in case of a violation of "essential elements." Such a structure creates the conditions under which human rights violations of a particular scale in partner countries could be qualified as a material breach of the treaty in terms of Article 60 of the Vienna Convention on the Law of Treaties and could justify the suspension of the treaty or the application of other countermeasures.[43] The first binding "essential element" clause was introduced in the 1995 revision of the EU-ACP Lomé Convention that distinguished the rule of law as an "essential element".[44] While not containing an "essential element" clause in its conventional form, the EU-Viet Nam FTA refers to the 2012 Framework Cooperation Agreement between contracting parties.[45] According to Article 1, democratic principles, human rights, and the rule of law represent "essential elements" under the Agreement. An important peculiarity of this norm is an emphasis on the relationship between international and domestic law, that requires Viet Nam's compliance with "the purposes and principles of the Charter of the United Nations..." and international human rights treaties.

Online Content Platform for Edward Elgar Publishing, November 27, 2015, https://www.elgaronline.com/view/edcoll/9781783477753/9781783477753.00005.xml.

[42] Tobias Dolle, "Human Rights Clauses in EU Trade Agreements: The New European Strategy in Free Trade Agreement Negotiations Focuses on Human Rights—Advantages and Disadvantages," in *The Influence of Human Rights on International Law* (Springer, Cham, 2015), 214.

[43] Vienna Convention on the law of treaties, U.N.T.S., 1155, I-18232.

[44] Agreement amending the Fourth ACP-EC Convention of Lomé, signed in Mauritius on 4 November 1995, OJ L 156/3 of 29 May 1998, Art. 5.

[45] EU-Vietnam Trade Agreement ("EU-Vietnam FTA"). https://trade.ec.europa.eu/doclib/press/index .cfm?id=1437; Framework Agreement on Comprehensive Partnership and Cooperation between the European Union and its Member States, of the one part, and the Socialist Republic of Viet Nam, of the other part. OJ L 329, 3.12.2016, pp. 8–42.

Article 1 also refers to "the commitment to further cooperate toward the full achievement of internationally agreed development goals..." as an "essential element." Article 2 of the Framework Agreement, highlighting the aims of cooperation, does not more broadly mention the rule of law and its components in the context of the advancement of trade and investment and economic cooperation. Instead, the rule of law is referred to as a part of the justice and security agenda, alongside legal cooperation, data protection, migration, and countering organized crime.

More importantly, most of the RTAs in question stipulate that a party's failure to provide administrative cooperation and report customs-related irregularities or fraud can result in the temporary suspension of preferential treatment.[46] As understood by the RTAs, the notions of customs irregularities or fraud encompass several breaches of the legality and legal certainty principles, such as customs authorities' "repeated failure to respect the obligations to verify the originating status of the product(s) concerned."[47] Moreover, the respective provisions emphasize the accountability and transparency dimensions of the rule of law by recognizing the authorities' "repeated refusal or undue delay in obtaining authorization to conduct administrative cooperation missions" as "a failure to provide administrative cooperation."[48] The fundamental instruments that the framework administrative cooperation standards utilize to promote the rule of law include the imposition of basic standards and consultations with the relevant treaty bodies.[49]

As opposed to framework norms on administrative cooperation, the RTAs' "Customs and Trade Facilitation" chapters are marked by the numerous rule of law standards. Compared to customs cooperation, trade facilitation is a broader

---

[46] EU-Kosovo SAA, Art. 48; EU-Ukraine AA, Art. 37(1); EU-CARIFORUM EPA, Art. 20(1).

[47] EU-Kosovo SAA, Art. 48(3); EU-Ukraine AA, Art. 37(3); EU-CARIFORUM EPA, Art. 20(3).

[48] *Ibid.*

[49] For instance, the Subcommittee on Customs, Trade Facilitation, and Rules of Origin as set by Art. 168 of the EU-Peru- Colombia FTA or the Trade Committee, according to Article 2.8 of the EU-Viet Nam FTA and a sanctions mechanism.

concept, encompassing an indefinite range of trade-related issues. Thus, it is more likely to generate spill overs in other issue areas. Accordingly, Article 75 of the EU-Ukraine DCFTA and Article 4.3.2(a) of the EU-Viet Nam FTA requires the parties' efforts in the customs cooperation and trade domain and aims to promote "legitimate trade." Nonetheless, the teleological analysis of the "Customs and Trade Facilitation" chapters under the EU-Ukraine DCFTA and the EU-Viet Nam FTA indicates that their objective is immediately concerned with the legality dimension of the rule of law. Consequently, Article 76 of the EU-Ukraine DCFTA and Art. 4.3.2(a) of the EU-Viet Nam FTA stipulates that legitimate trade protection requires "effective enforcement of and compliance with legislative requirements."

3. Economic Integration and Domestic Law Reform in Viet Nam

Viet Nam has experienced 34 years of market-oriented reforms in conjunction with international economic integration since Doi Mo (Economic Renovation) was launched in December 1986. The resulting socio-economic achievements were impressive - from a poor country, Viet Nam has now reached a lower-middle-income economy. The country initiated trade negotiations once it became an official member of the Association of South East Asian Nations (ASEAN) in 1995. A year later, in January 1996, it joined the ASEAN Free Trade Area (AFTA), the first FTA of Viet Nam. 2007 marked a significant milestone when Viet Nam became the 150th Member of the WTO. This opportunity provided comprehensive steps toward trade and investment liberalization, alongside economic reform. Also, 2015 has remained highly successful as it signed four RTAs with some of its largest trading partners, namely the EU (EVFTA), South Korea, Eurasia Economic Union (EEC), and Comprehensive and Progressive Trans-Pacific Partnership (CPTPP).[50] By April 2020, Viet Nam has signed 13

---

[50] CPTPP had a total of 11 members, including Australia, Brunei, Canada, Chile, Malaysia,

FTAs, and all of them have already come into effect. Prominently, Viet Nam signed five FTAs as an ASEAN member and the rest as an independent country. The establishment of the ASEAN Economic Community as a replacement of AFTA in 2016 could enhance the regional cooperation for Viet Nam. Moreover, Viet Nam's effort to integrate its economy with the rest of the world is also marking it as an FTA hub in South East Asia, presently a strategic region globally.

Like other nations, the underlying economic benefits have played a vital role in Viet Nam's efforts to participate in many FTAs in a relatively short time. Moreover, the FTA drive seems to have paid off in the form of increased trade and FDI. A study argues that exporters in Viet Nam have benefited from the enlargement of export markets and reduced tariff and non-tariff barriers, thanks to FTAs.[51] Viet Nam was also given more extended implementation periods for tariff reduction and elimination compared to ASEAN-6 (Brunei, Indonesia, Malaysia, Phillipines, Thailand, and Singapore) and its FTA partners. Presently, Viet Nam is linked with the largest trading partners and the primary FDI sources by the FTAs, such as the EU, Japan, Korea, China. Nonetheless, a look at the constituents of FTAs reveals Viet Nam's both trade and international relations strategies that diversify and multilateralize external relations. For example, Viet Nam focuses on regional and geographically scale as well as traditional markets through FTAs. Also, its FTA partners are at different levels of development and have less similar trade structures. In the medium to long run, Viet Nam would improve its domestic and international competitiveness and reduce its dependence on any single trade partner, as is China's case at present. Besides, through those agreements, Viet Nam has been recognized as a full market economy by many countries, including India, Australia, and New Zealand.[52]

However, the active participation of Viet Nam in the trade agreement has

---

Mexico, New Zealand, Japan, Peru, Singapore, and Viet Nam. The USA has withdrawn from the deal in 2016.

[51] Asia Regional Integration Center, *Viet Nam's Participation in Free Trade Agreements: History and the Way Forward*, 4.

[52] Ibid.

not remained free of challenges. Although various institutional reforms that Viet Nam has enacted so far to become an FTA partner with other economies should have a long-term positive impact on its future development, its participation in new-generation FTAs, specifically, has created several challenges for both economy and institutional reforms. The quality and coverage of these FTAs have evolved continually to cover various fields, far beyond the traditional ones. Some of Viet Nam's FTAs, such as EVFTA and CPTPP, now cover primary sectors such as trade in goods, services, and investment and the extent to which non-economic issues such as intellectual property, government spending, competitive policies, labor, and environmental standards The improvement of industry-specific performance, economic competitiveness, labor, and environmental standards is difficult and time-consuming. The decline in tax revenue due to various tariff reduction commitments to the FTAs is emerging to be an issue for the government. Therefore, Viet Nam could be a good case study for its effort to transform from a socialist economy to a market-based socialist economy where globalization and trade agreements have become an instrument of transition.

Many authors believed that trade agreements positively impact legal and institutional reforms and improve the national image and position of Viet Nam in the international infrastructure.[53] The commitments under FTAs require the country to comply with international rules and standards and revise the national legal system and government regulations toward a transparent business climate and fairer competition to attract foreign investors and trading partners. One of the fundamental reforms in preparing for joining FTAs was the revision of trade and tax policies. Before 2000, Viet Nam employed an "import substitution" trade policy; even the government had no tariff elimination schedule or reduction. However, since 2001, Viet Nam has pursued the export-oriented trade policy to

---

[53] See generally Vo Tri Thanh, "Vietnam's Perspectives on Regional Economic Integration," *Journal of Southeast Asian Economies* 32, no. 1 (2015): 106–24; and Nguyen Trinh Thanh Nguyen, "The Reform of Vietnamese Economic Institutions under the Impact of Free Trade Agreements A Case Study of the EU and Vietnam Free Trade Agreement," *Köz-gazdaság - Review of Economic Theory and Policy* 13, no. 3 (2018): 191–203.

join WTO and participate in AFTA and other FTAs. To meet these requirements, Viet Nam has restricted its policy space, especially trade protectionism policies, through domestic companies' protection mechanisms such as tariff and non-tariff barriers.[54]

Additionally, Viet Nam amended and adopted a new Import-Export Tariff Law in 2005, which had the largest number of amendments. The new law high-lighted the government obligations of implementing tariff reduction and elimina-tion commitments under FTAs. Viet Nam's List of Preferential Tariff is updated every year to comply with the FTA commitments. For example, after signing a new-generation FTA with EU and joining CPTPP, the Vietnamese Commercial Law of 2005 is proposed to be revised to be compatible with FTAs commitments. In line with these trade policy changes, the government also amended the fiscal policy by increasing spending, especially infrastructure.[55]

However, as mentioned above, participation in various trade agreements, especially new-generation FTAs, also imposes many challenges to Viet Nam. When joining the FTAs, the significant challenge for Viet Nam is institutional reforms, which influence the investment environment. Unlike other economies, Viet Nam has been practicing a socialist-oriented market economy. However, this economic model's definition is vague and incomplete, and it is unclear how the "socialist element" can manipulate the current market economy and how to implement this strategy. Besides that, Viet Nam's current economic model is far from the model of a full market economy because of the clash between characteristics of the "socialist factor" and basic principles of a market economy such as supply and demand, competition, and price mechanisms.[56] Likewise,

---

[54] National Institute for Finance, *Facilitate the Policy Space to Support Vietnam's Domestic Enterprises after Signing FTAs. NIF Portal* (July 27, 2015).

[55] T.D Tuyen et al., *Impacts of Market Liberalization Requirements under WTO and FTAs on Production, Trade and Measures to Perfect the Import–export Management Mechanisms of Ministry of Industry and Trade 2011–2015*, Ha Noi, MUTRAP III Report (September 2011).

[56] See Phan Quan Viet, "Opportunities and Challenges When Vietnam Joins TPP," *Issues in Economics and Business* 2, no. 1 (2016): 28–46.

in recent years, state-owned enterprises have received many favors over other business types. Thus, FTAs commitments have led to immense pressure to foster and complete state-owned enterprises' reform process. Mainly, CPTPP has introduced the regulations on the duration for state-owned enterprises reform to ensure transparency (in the valuation of assets as well as transparency in the business operation), transformation (focus on quality, corporate structure rather than quantity, the number of equitized enterprises) and comprehensiveness (not to ignore or bias any enterprises).[57]

Another significant issue is the pressure for reforming economic legislation. The Competition Law has been put into force since 2004 and amended in 2014 but still has many flaws and legal loopholes. For example, this law's scope limits the competitive behaviors of entities operating within Viet Nam's territory without mentioning the competitive behaviors of entities operating outside but have effects on Viet Nam's market. Moreover, the government published Competition Law under international economic integration pressure rather than under the market's pressure. In terms of the specific commitments to the Trade and Sustainable Development Chapter in EVFTA, although the Agreement has been approved and gradually comes into force, Viet Nam will have to continue its efforts to adopt many international standards. Later, it will need to ensure enforcement and support affected people in society to meet commitments and make the best use of this Agreement's trade growth opportunities. Specifically for labor commitments, the National Assembly has recently passed a revised Labor Code with changes consistent with both CPTPP and EVFTA. The revised Labor Code currently included the contents of the ILO's Conventions, but the government will also have to draft detailed guidelines in its implementing regulations. Besides, the Trade Union Law will also have to be amended to comply with ILO regulations. Simultaneously, the government needs to have effective mechanisms that closely monitor the implementation of regulations to bridge the gap between

---

[57] T.H.P Dao, "The Implementation of TPP: Needs Government Support to Take Advantage of New Markets. Research Forum on Ministry of Finance Website," March 16, 2016.

policy regulations and policy implementation, especially those on labor safety enforcements.

According to the Global Competitiveness Report 2015–2016 of the WEF, Viet Nam is ranked 56th out of 140 countries on competitiveness and business environment. Although this ranking has marked a significant improvement, from 68th in 2014, Viet Nam is still lagging behind its ASEAN counterparts. Viet Nam also has the lowest position among the essential element index, listed at the 85th position out of 140 countries and eighth over ten in ASEAN countries. The figure demonstrates the most critical indicators of an institution that play a decisive role in Viet Nam's competitiveness.[58] Viet Nam is still standing poorly on the score list. Among these indicators, "Irregular payments and bribe" has the lowest position with the rank of 106th/140, followed by the "Strength of investors' protection" and "Burdens from government procurement," ranked 100th and 90th, respectively. This result suggests that Viet Nam's administrative procedures are still complicated, time-consuming, and costly for enterprises. Inevitably, this contributes to limited public service quality, an increase in irregular payments, corruption, and harassment toward businesses and investors, making the business environment and economy less transparent, less attractive, and less competitive.

Bibliography

Agénor, Pierre-Richard. *Does Globalization Hurt the Poor?* The World Bank. 2002.

Asia Regional Integration Center. *Viet Nam's Participation in Free Trade Agreements: History and the Way Forward.* Accessed November 15, 2020.

Baier, Scott L., Jeffrey H. Bergstrand, Peter Egger, and Patrick A. McLaughlin. "Do Economic Integration Agreements Actually Work? Issues in Understanding the Causes and Consequences of the Growth of Regionalism." *World Economy* 31, no. 4 (2008): 461–497.

---

[58] World Economic Forum, *Global Competitiveness Report 2015–2016*, (2016).

Baldwin, Richard E. "Multilateralising Regionalism: Spaghetti Bowls as Building Blocs on the Path to Global Free Trade." *World Economy* 29, no. 11 (2006): 1451–1518.

Barr, Michael S., and Geoffrey P. Miller. "Global Administrative Law: The View from Basel." *European Journal of International Law* 17, no. 1 (2006): 15–46.

Battersby, Paul. *The Unlawful Society: Global Crime and Security in a Complex World.* Springer. 2014.

Börzel, Tanja A., and Thomas Risse. "Introduction: Framework of the Handbook and Conceptual Clarifications." In *The Oxford Handbook of Comparative Regionalism*, edited by Tanja Börzel and Thomas Risse, 3–15. Oxford University Press. 2016.

Bossche, Peter Van den, and Werner Zdouc. *The Law and Policy of the World Trade Organization: Text, Cases and Materials.* Cambridge University Press. 2017.

Braithwaite, John. *Regulatory Capitalism: How It Works, Ideas for Making It Work Better.* Edward Elgar Publishing. 2008.

Carothers, Thomas. "The Rule of Law Revival." *Foreign Aff.* 77 (1998): 95.

Carpenter, Theresa. "A Historical Perspective on Regionalism." In *Multilateralizing Regionalism: Challenges for the Global Trading System*, edited by Richard Baldwin and Patrick Low, 13–27. Cambridge University Press. 2009.

Dao, T.H.P. "The Implementation of TPP: Needs Government Support to Take Advantage of New Markets. Research Forum on Ministry of Finance Website," March 16, 2016. http://moj.gov.vn/qt/tintuc/Pages/nghien-cuu- trao-doi.aspx?ItemID=1937.

Davis, Kevin E., and Michael J. Trebilcock. "The Relationship between Law and Development: Optimists versus Skeptics." *The American Journal of Comparative Law* 56, no. 4 (2008): 895–946.

Desierto, Diane A. "The International Mandate for Development: Building Compliant Investment within the State's Development Decision-Making Processes." In *International Investment Law and Development.* Edward Elgar Publishing. 2015.

Dolle, Tobias. "Human Rights Clauses in EU Trade Agreements: The New European Strategy in Free Trade Agreement Negotiations Focuses on Human Rights—Advantages and Disadvantages." In *The Influence of Human Rights on International Law*, 213–28. Springer, Cham. 2015.

Fawcett, Louise. "Exploring Regional Domains: A Comparative History of Regionalism." *International Affairs* 80, no. 3 (2004): 429–446.

Friedman, Thomas L. *The Lexus and the Olive Tree.* HarperCollins. 2000.

Fuller, Lon L. *The Morality of Law.* Yale University Press. 1964.

Haas, Ernst B. *Beyond the Nation State: Functionalism and International Organization.* ECPR Press. 2008.

Haas, Ernst B., and Desmond Dinan. *The Uniting of Europe: Political, Social, and Economic Forces, 1950–1957.* Vol. 311. Stanford University Press. 1958.

Kessie, E. K. "The World Trade Organization and Regional Trade Agreements : An Analysis of the Relevant Rules of the WTO." Sydney. Thesis. The University of Technology, Doctor of Juridical Science. 2001. https://opus.lib.uts.edu.au/handle/10453/20254.

Kim, Joy A. "Harnessing Regional Trade Agreements for the Post-2012 Climate Change Regime." *Climate and Trade*, 2009, 57.

Leal-Arcas, Rafael. "Proliferation of Regional Trade Agreements: Complementing or Supplanting Multilateralism." *Chi. J. Int'l L.* 11 (2010–2011): 597–630.

Marx, Axel, Bregt Natens, Dylan Geraets, and Jan Wouters. "Global Governance through Trade: An Introduction." *Elgar Online: The Online Content Platform for Edward Elgar Publishing*, November 27, 2015. https://www.elgaronline.com/view/edcoll/9781783477753/9781783477753.00005.xml.

Miller, Arthur Selwyn. "The Global Corporation and American Constitutionalism: Some Political Consequences of Economic Power." *J. Int'l L. & Econ.* 6 (1971): 235.

Mitrany, David. "A Working Peace System." In *The European Union*, 77–97. Palgrave, London. 1994.

National Institute for Finance. *Facilitate the Policy Space to Support Vietnam's Domestic Enterprises after Signing FTAs. NIF Portal*, July 27, 2015.

Nguyen, Nguyen Trinh Thanh. "The Reform of Vietnamese Economic Institutions under the Impact of Free Trade Agreements A Case Study of the EU and Vietnam Free Trade Agreement." *Köz-gazdaság - Review of Economic Theory and Policy* 13, no. 3 (2018): 191–203.

OECD. *Foreign Direct Investment for Development*, 2002.

Ohmae, Kenichi. "The Borderless World." *McKinsey Quarterly*, no. 3 (1990): 3–19.

Rabinovych, Maryna. "Where Economic Development Meets the Rule of Law? Promoting Sustainable Development Goals Through the European Neighborhood Policy." *Brill Open Law* 2, no. 1 (April 3, 2020): 140–74.

Raz, Joseph. "The Rule of Law and Its Virtue, The Authority of Law: Essays on Law and Morality." *Oxford: Oxford University Press* 210 (1979): 221–2.

Ridgway, Delissa A., and Mariya A. Talib. "Globalization and Development - Free Trade, Foreign Aid, Investment and the Rule of Law Essay." *Cal. W. Int'l L.J.* 33, no. 2 (2002–2003): 325–44.

Söderbaum, Fredrik. "Early, Old, New and Comparative Regionalism: The Scholarly Development of the Field." *KFG Working Paper Series* no. 64, Kolleg-Forschergruppe (KFG) "The Transformative Power of Europe" (2015). https://ssrn.com/abstract=2687942

Srinivasan, Thirukodikaval N., and Jessica Seddon Wallack. "Globalization, Growth, and the Poor." *De Economist* 152, no. 2 (2004): 251–72.

Stiglitz, Joseph. *Globalization and Its Discontents*. Penguin UK. 2015.

Strange, Susan, and Scholar of International Relations Susan Strange. *The Retreat of the State: The Diffusion of Power in the World Economy*. Cambridge University Press. 1996.

Tamanaha, Brian Z. "The Primacy of Society and the Failures of Law and Development." *Cor-*

nell Int'l LJ 44 (2011): 209.

Thanh, Vo Tri. "Vietnam's Perspectives on Regional Economic Integration." *Journal of Southeast Asian Economies* 32, no. 1 (2015): 106–24.

Tuyen, T.D., V.T. Thanh, B.T. Giang, P.V. Chinh, L.T. Dung, N.A. Duong, and N.D. Thanh. *Impacts of Market Liberalization Requirements under WTO and FTAs on Production, Trade and Measures to Perfect the Import–export Management Mechanisms of Ministry of Industry and Trade 2011–2015*. Ha Noi, MUTRAP III Report. September 2011.

Vadi, Valentina Sara. "Access to Medicines versus Protection of 'Investments' in Intellectual Property: Reconciliation through Interpretation?" *Law in the Pursuit of Development: Principles into Practice?*, 2009, 52.

Viet, Phan Quan. "Opportunities and Challenges When Vietnam Joins TPP." *Issues in Economics and Business* 2, no. 1 (2016): 28–46.

Wade, Robert. "Globalization and Its Limits: Reports of the Death of the National Economy Are Greatly Exaggerated." *National Diversity and Global Capitalism* 8 (1996): 60–88.

Wolf, Martin. "Globalisation." *Financial Times*, June 13, 2013. https://www.ft.com/content/12c74980-d1bf-11e2-9336-00144feab7de.

World Economic Forum. *Global Competitiveness Report 2015–2016*, 2016.

PART II

THE RULE OF LAW PROMOTION AND THE ROLE OF UNIVERSITY IN ASIA*

Participants

Thailand

Hattapong Hirunt (Thammasat Univ.)

Laos

Latdavanh Donkeodavong (National Univ. of Laos)

Cambodia

Mao Kimpav (Paññāsāstra Univ.)

Tharin Vong (Paññāsāstra Univ.)

Vietnam

Phan Thi Lan Huong (Hanoi Law Univ.)

Tran Khanh Van (Lawyer, Keio Law School Alumini)

Nepal

Aman Maharjan (Private Attorney)

Japan

Rikako Watai (Keio Law School)

Toshitaka Kudo (Keio Law School)

Shohei Sugita (Lawyer)

Yosuke Kobayashi (JICA)

Hitomi Fukasawa (KEIGLAD; Keio Law School)

Moderator

Hiroshi Matsuo (KEIGLAD; Keio Law School)

---

* The following is the record of discussion at the Programs for Asian Global Legal Professions (PAGLEP) Symposium 2020: University's Contribution toward "the Rule of Law Ubiquitous World" held on November 21, 2020, by way of the Internet.

Hiroshi Matsuo:

In the morning's presentation session, we have confirmed the meaning of the rule of law through concrete issues such as how to improve access to government information and legal sources, how to strengthen legal protections for children and workers by prescribing them in substantive and procedural laws, and providing dispute resolution systems for them. We have also learned how to fill the gap between international rules and domestic laws by raising citizens' interest in what their laws should be. Then, there are people's increasing concerns with what is meant by the rule of law. The most crucial common recognition is that the rule of law cannot be understood abstractly, in a static form, and by mere observation. Instead, we should capture it under a country's unique conditions, in its dynamic development process, and by our participation to a part of that process.

From these presentations, what do you think is the primary driver of promoting the rule of law in our countries? Is it new legislation by the government, or is it international pressures? Is it a reflection of the people's economic interests or of the internal interests of stakeholder populations such as students, workers, business persons, or other society members? Universities can promote the rule of law through studying the concept including how to implement it and how to facilitate it.

One particular contribution of universities is fostering students to be intermediaries between the legal system and civil society from a global perspective. In the future students can be stewards of the law, by interpreting legal terms, translating the meanings of our legal rules and theories, and explaining the aims of the law so that ordinary people can comprehend its purpose. In the afternoon sessions, I'd like to discuss how to foster students who have a global perspective and global approaches to the difficult issues that globalizing societies face today.

Since the Keio Law School's Program for Fostering Asian Global Legal Professions (PAGLEP: [http://keiglad.keio.ac.jp/en/paglep/]) started five

years ago, more than 220 students have participated in the program, and I think they are the most important outcome of our joint project. But to contribute to the promotion of the rule of law, we need to improve the program, and we would like to ask you how we can do that. Before we start taking any comments or questions, I'd like to ask Professor Watai to give us a brief introduction to the Keio Law School, which established the English LL.M. programs for students who come from all over the world. Some law schools in our partner universities have already established English language law programs. But what are the advantages and aims of legal instruction in English? May I ask Professor

Watai to give us an introduction to the Keio Law School LL.M. course?

Rikako Watai:

Professor Matsuo, thank you for giving me the opportunity to speak about the education at Keio University Law School. My name is Rikako Watai, and I'm a professor of administrative law; and I currently serve as the director of the LL.M. program in global legal practice. In the age of globalization, I think the rule of law has value and that it is especially important to share this value, and universities can do a lot in this area.

Let's go back in time a little. Keio's legal education goes as far back as

1890; the first head of the law department was John Henry Wigmore, a famous evidence law professor from the United States who was recruited as a foreign advisor to the Japanese government. Professor Wigmore stayed with us for two years, and his students succeeded him. In this classroom picture from the early 1920s, you can recognize legal terms written on the blackboard like "equity." Japan introduced the U.S.-style law school system in 2004, and our LL.M program started in 2017. Keio has always been a home for comparative legal studies, and this is one way we share our views on the rule of law. Now we have the honor of collaborating with you all, which means now Keio is as global as ever.

The students who enter the Keio LL.M. course include qualified lawyers as well as those who have completed law school and want to improve their English competencies and practical skills in English. We also aim to train students who will be globally active legal professionals. Our program will open its doors to newly graduates who wish to work in international organizations. We welcome exchange students with interest in Japanese or Asian law. Here at Keio, students from all these different backgrounds can come together to exchange their perspectives on how we apply the rule of law.

The Keio LL.M. degree program requires that students complete at least 30 credits. The standard duration for completiing the course is one year, and students may begin their studies in either April or September. All students must earn at least four credits in either global business law or global security law and at least four credits of practical training. Global business law courses cover international transactions and international dispute resolution, and global security law deals with human rights, environmental law, and security issues. The practical training involves applied learning, including mock trials and internships at law offices and corporate legal departments. These flexible requirements allow students to create programs that meet their individual needs. Then there are the elective courses covering the legal systems in Asian countries and the latest issues happening in the law. The program here offers value for both theory and practice.

The program offers certificates in business law, intellectual property law, international dispute resolution, Japanese law, and most important of all, law and development in Asia. Each certificate requires satisfactory completion of at least 10 credits in the relevant field, as well as a two-credit research paper. Of course, you can choose not to seek a certificate and instead just take the courses that interest you. You can study broadly or in-depth, and this is very new for us.

On February 21st, 2019, Keio University Law School qualified as a recognized course provider for the Chartered Institute of Arbitrators (CIArb). The CIArb is based in London and is a leading institution for dispute management. From April 2019, students who completed classes Introduction to Arbitration, International Commercial Arbitration and Mediation could qualify as CIArb members.

Finally, the background of our new

LL.M program is globalization. Our goal is to train Japanese and foreign lawyers to be global players, and I think this is what universities can do to promote the rule of law. Globalization is deeply connected to education, and we have high expectations for working with you all in promoting rule of law. I hope we can get together sometime in the near future and next time in person. Thank you very much.

Hiroshi Matsuo:

Thank you, Professor Watai for giving us a really good guide to the Keio LL.M course in just five minutes, one example of our challenges in providing law instruction including Asian law in English. Other universities have had similar intentions and faced similar challenges, and we need to improve our joint programs for the future.

Today, I'm very glad to see the names of students who have participated in the PAGLEP or who graduated LL.M. course. If you have any comments, requests, or questions for how we can improve our programs, please feel free to give us based on your experience. Professor Huong, do you have any comments?

Phan Thi Lan Huong:

Yes, thank you Professor Matsuo. I would like to share some of my ideas about developing the English program. It's very important in the globalization context and very different from the way of Vietnam like Hanoi Law University. We also hope that we can have some English programs for most undergraduate and LL.M. students, but so far it's quite challenging because we face many difficulties. The first is we lack the human resources, professors who can give the lectures in English. The second is we also lack training documents in English; for example, there are very few books written in English.

We are now considering developing an LL.M. program. Without that, we cannot promote exchange programs with partner universities like Keio University. I think that you just mentioned about teaching the law in English. From my own experience, at Nagoya University, they have an ASEAN law course, and they invite professors from partner universities to give lectures on topics related to countries such as Vietnam and Cambodia. Using the advantages of online technologies, it's easy for you to organize courses on ASEAN law by inviting professors from partner universities to give lectures like that.

One more similar topic you mentioned today is about the role of universities in promoting the rule of law. I share the viewpoint that we create in law school graduates intermediate human resources who play important roles in law enforcement not only as lawyers but also as judges and public prosecutors. They will become key persons in the enforcement system. Also for law school today, I think that for the rule of law in society, we need to protect human rights and provide legal support for the people.

Also in Vietnam for example, universities play an important role in the legislative enactment, because through conferences and workshops, scholars and professors give a lot of comments and input in drafting laws. I think that the role of the university in promoting the rule of law state is very important not only for Vietnam but I think for other countries through developing human resources and also giving input through research. One more point is that in terms of common use of the term "rule of law" in Asian countries, every country has different legal contexts and cultures. So laws and law enforcement are influenced by many factors like politics, cultures, and beliefs and also by globalization, like Professor Dao Gia Phuc also shared from Vietnam.

Now our domestic laws have to be reformed to conform to international standards, and we had to narrow the gap between our legal system and the international standard. So coming back to law school, the law professors played important roles in the research to identify legal issue and the gaps between domestic and international laws. I think it's been a very informative workshop today, and thank you for inviting us to join this workshop.

Hiroshi Matsuo:

Thank you very much, Professor Huong. The university's role is not

limited to foster human resources who will be engaged in drafting laws. Still, it will also contribute to the legislative process by deliberating a draft and commenting on it or providing comparative law information in the development process. As for the possible extension of the English programs network, I think we have a lot of potential in the Asian region. Today, we have a guest from Nepal. Mr. Aman Maharjan, can you hear me?

Namaste! Mr. Aman graduated from the University of Tribhuvan and the Kathmandu Law School if my memory is correct. The Kathmandu Law School also provides legal subjects in English. May I ask some questions? What do you think are the advantages or the strengths of your law school in providing legal subjects in English? And do you have some ideas for improving the programs?

Aman Maharjan:

Thank you, Professor Matsuo. I graduated from the Tribhuvan University. The course we studied was, in bachelors, it was five years BA.LL.B. and in LL.M. We could choose various different subjects, such as our constitutional law, commercial law, international law, and environment law as well. I would say that the course being in English language was very beneficial to us because it made us capable of being competitive in this global legal arena. But certain things, what I felt was that a few things needed to be studied in Nepal itself because the court language in Nepal is in Nepali, and it was very essential for us to study procedural law at least in Nepali that would prepare us to go into the practice.

So all in all, it was English medium for us, and it was very beneficial because there were a lot of resource books and reference materials available in English. I really found that the syllabus we had needed improvement. They made some reforms in changing to the semester system. Nonetheless, I would still say we need a lot of reforms in the syllabus itself, so that the students can learn more, learn more that can help them to understand the law in the global perspective.

Hiroshi Matsuo:

Thank you very much, Mr. Aman. That is a very informative comment. Can I ask further? What kind of subjects are taught in English? Like business law or human rights or contracts?

Aman Maharjan:

Actually, we had one Nepali subject that was legal Nepali; everything else is taught in English. We have human rights subjects. In our bachelor's, we had to study economics, sociology, anthropology, history even, and almost everything was taught in English. In the master's, there is no Nepali subject. Everything is taught in English. We have to take our exams in English. I would say Nepal pretty much has English medium legal education.

Hiroshi Matsuo:

Thank you very much. This is also very interesting information. In the last comment, Professor Huong from Hanoi Law University also talked about some difficulties in sharing materials which are not written in English. We could share the materials, and we could then also share human resources, if we can improve the joint programs. They will also provide legal information about different cultures, different political backgrounds, and different reactions to globalization. We can learn a lot from the various patterns of our legal reform in accordance with the changing social conditions. Thank you very much, Mr. Aman.

Aman Maharjan:

Thank you so much.

Hitomi Fukasawa:

Today, I found many students and former students who participated in Keio University Law School programs. We talk about how universities contribute to promoting the rule of law. In my opinion, to think about the role of university, it is necessary to get feedback from students. Because in other words, students are the outcomes from a university's legal education. I would like to ask former students about what they learned about the rule of law in university and how they feel about the rule of law in a real society?

Hiroshi Matsuo:

Professor Watai, do you have some comments?

Rikako Watai:

I wanted to make a comment to Professor Huong's remarks, and I also share the same issue: It's very hard to find professors who would teach Japanese law in English. I'd like to have more Japanese law courses offered in our LL.M program. There are not many Japanese laws translated into English, and Japanese administrative law relies heavily on case law even though Japan is a civil law country. And not many cases are translated into English either. I think it would help to have the Japanese government promote the translation of Japanese law into English. That would help us very much, and I think there's much we can do as scholars contribute to that work.

Hiroshi Matsuo:

Thank you, Professor Watai. I agree with your comment. We have room to improve the further provision of English materials on national laws to share the information.

Latdavanh Donkeodavong:

Hello Professor.

Hiroshi Matsuo:

Yes, please, Dr. Latdavanh.

Latdavanh Donkeodavong:

Can I ask more information related to Professor Watai? She mentioned resources in English. I graduated from Nagoya University, and I did the comparative study by learning from the administrative law of Japan, the state compensation, administrative case litigation. The problem is that some legal sources are not translated in English. The national diet has some sources and the Supreme Court, they have some website to download judgments, such as the Minamata disease case and the Itai-Itai disease case, whatever.

There are many cases, but the problem is there are some laws like local autonomy laws that have no official translation. It would be good if the government of Japan or the Ministry of Justice of Japan translated the local autonomy laws and many laws that have not yet been translated. In the field of administrative law, it's really helpful for us, for me too. I'm interested in Japanese law and try to introduce the Japanese to the Ministry of Justice and Laws. Right now, many agencies like JICA and the Luxembourg University support us to draft the law to help the Ministry of Justice, but the problem is some laws are not translated yet. So it would be good to translate and it would be helpful for us.

Rikako Watai:

I agree with you. Those basic laws such as local or autonomy law don't have official translations, and also the case laws as you mentioned... There's a supreme court website that has English translations of famous recent cases but not old cases, and so many important cases are still under interpretation and have not been translated yet. And even those cases that do have translation, I think, are very hard to understand. I don't think the translation is easy to follow. Of course, it's difficult to translate specific administrative law terms into English.

Hiroshi Matsuo:

Thank you, Dr. Latdavanh and Professor Watai. Professor Huong may have some further comments.

Phan Thi Lan Huong:

I'd like to share a little bit about the translated documents. I would like to share that it is the most challenging for us when we study law in Japan, because assets are legal documents in English, we can find some in Japan. They have one translation, the English translation, the website; it's not official but you can refer. But it is quite challenging for foreign students in the English training program because of legal terms, and how we understand the legal terms in the law context is very important. As in the Vietnamese case, in translating our laws into English, we sometimes cannot find similar terms in legal English because they are heavily influenced by politics and by our system.

It's like the common issue for the Asian countries because we use our own languages, so it's quite challenging, but like Professor Matsuo mentioned, we can have some kind of common understanding, and we can

develop the common terms to use in Asian countries under the rule of law standard. Thank you.

Hiroshi Matsuo:

Thank you very much, Professor Huong, Professor Watai, and Dr. Latdavanh. Translating legal documents and legal text is very hard, but also it is a very interesting process because we can compare the similar terms but different meanings. So this itself is a very good example of the study of law. We can understand how the law is deeply rooted in the social context, social history, so that if we have similar terms, it does not necessarily mean it has the same meaning. We need to understand the little but important differences between similar legal terms to deepen our mutual understanding and avoid misunderstanding of the mutual laws. Anyway, thank you very much for providing us a problem of translation of the legal texts written in national languages. I think all the comments concerned with the translation of the legal terms, legal thoughts and legal theories in national languages are very important.

Hitomi Fukasawa:

Professor Matsuo, while we are talking about the English translation issues, I got some questions and comments from Mr. Tharin Vong and Ms. Tran Khanh Van. Can I ask them? Mr. Tharin, can you go first?

Tharin Vong:

Yes, I can go first.

Okay. I think Professor Watai has mentioned an interesting point about case law. But let me introduce myself first. My name is Tharin. I'm a fresh graduate student from Paññāsāstra University of Cambodia, and I started working as a legal assistant in a law office in 2018. Through my experiences as a legal assistant and a student, I started to realize that what is necessary to understand is not only the law but also the facts of the case, particularly the fact that constitutes the right and liability under the scope, meaning, and purposes of the law.

In practice, we have to utilize and comprehend both the law and the fact together; if we cannot understand the fact clearly, we also cannot apply the law correctly. By this reasoning, the case law, which usually includes the summary fact of the case, applied provisions of the law, reasons for the decision, and the final decision made by judges, is unique studying material to provide realities of both the fact and the applied law. Otherwise, as a student with experience I spent most of my time only studying the law with few examples of actual facts of the cases mentioned by the lecturers. During class, I felt that I was lacking comprehension of the facts related to law that I studied in class, which made it difficult for me to analyze, address, and differentiate the important facts from the non–relevant facts that occurred in the real cases when I started working. Related to this problem, I come up with a particular form of education that can be effectively applied that students in classes should have chances to read the case law as much possible so that they can understand both the fact of the case and the law. By doing so, the students will be able to learn how to address and differentiate what facts should be taken into account under the scope, meaning, and purpose of law when encountering long facts being described by the disputed parties and mountains of documentary evidence to read and analyze. I think doing this will benefit them as students when they start working in legal careers. So this is a form of educational reform that I think the university can apply, and in fact, it's very beneficial to Cambodian students if universities in Cambodia can apply this form of education.

Understanding case law helps students to understand the connections between the fact and law and also promote the effectiveness and efficiency of law practice when students start working in the legal world. In the context of Cambodia, some difficulties faced when compiling case law for university students to study are the limited sources and non-publicity of issuance of case law; students are not allowed or provided case law to read during class except in very limited cases because the judgment or case law is issued, used, and placed only in the court. Furthermore, only those who are working in the court and the law firm can read these cases due to privacy and confidentiality.

Departing from difficulties facing with accessing case law and judgments issued by the court, there is a good sign that today the Arbitration Council of Cambodia is making effort to compile the case law so that students and the public can access all those previous decisions or awards in order to read and understand both the fact of the case and applied provisions of the law in the context of labor dispute resolution. Moreover, the decision or award is issued publicly and can be found in both Khmer and English on the website of the Arbitration Council for free. Otherwise, it is not enough because as the law students, we would like to know not only the particular field of labor but other fields including commercial, civil, and criminal fields. So in general, there are still limited sources and availability of case law for the students to study during their classes in the universities, and it's a big challenge for them to sit down again in the workplace trying to learn and understand the fact of the case before deciding which law is appropriate to apply. Thank you, professor.

Hiroshi Matsuo:

Thank you, Mr. Tharin. This is also a very crucial topic. To publish the case law, it is very important and indispensable information to know correctly the content of law in each country. In the morning session, Professor Huong introduced us to the publication of the case law in Vietnam, which started in 2016, and this concerns the rule of law topic, especially the access to information or access to the legal sources, which Dr. Latdavanh also indicated. How we can improve this? How we can request the government to publish the case law information while avoiding infringing on the privacy and the confidentiality of the parties? We can ask the government to provide the case law information by anonymity. I think we cannot avoid this crucial topic to improve the rule of law. Thank you very much for indicating this important topic, Mr. Tharin.

Hitomi Fukasawa:

Professor Matsuo, I would like to invite Ms. Van, the Alumni of Keio LL.M student.

Tran Khanh Van:

I graduated from the Keio Law School LL.M program in 2018, and I'm now working for a Japanese bank that has branches in Hanoi. I think the bank has branches in many countries all over the world. The course is really helpful for me because I learned to view concepts from different legal perspectives, and international transaction is very, very popular in my daily work. I just have one comment and question to Professor Huong. In Vietnam, the court aside from the case has not been published, and we think that the judges are not very well trained in specific fields, especially for fields such as banking and finance that require very deep professional knowledge. Occasionally, a practitioner even needs to be consulted. For example, the State Bank of Vietnam and the state bank officials themselves need trainings and study with other professionals in other countries.

It is not very practical to require that judges in Vietnam have the knowledge to comprehend different concepts in fields such as banking and finance. This would mean that when a case in banking and finance is brought before the court, we struggle to rely on them, on their judgment of what terms mean in a contract regarding concepts they are not professional in. In such cases, it's very difficult. We would go to the state bank, and we would collect opinions, but Vietnamese law does not require that the court rely on the comments and opinions of professional officials such as the State Bank or even state authorities. How about the case in Japan? Because I think that not all judges are expert in every field, and some very specific fields require deep knowledge such as banking and finance. When a case is fought before the court, how do you deal with such issue that judges should be expert but they are not and their opinion has decisive meaning to the party?

Hiroshi Matsuo:

Thank you, Ms. Van. I understand very well about the problem and the situation; it is very difficult to answer. Sometimes, in a specific law field, for which expertized knowledge is required, like intellectual property law, there are some judges who are en-

gaged, especially in such kind of field. The special court can be established as well. But except for such field, the judges can cover or are required to cover any cases. Some judges cover the general and the special civil cases, and the other judges cover criminal cases. It depends on the legal education system for legal professions but I think it would be improved in the long run by continuing and improving the legal education system for professions.

But at the same time, lawyers need to provide some information with evidences. They are presented in the trial by the parties or the lawyers who support the parties. The continuous communication between the judges and the lawyers for the parties may gradually break through the situation. It maybe the collaboration or the cooperation between the judges and the lawyers for the parties. Any comments to answer Ms. Van's questions?

Rikako Watai:

I just wanted to make one comment. There are thousands of laws in Japan and judges are not experts in every field. I agree with her on this point. I think that complaint system, established by the Administrative Complaint Review Act, would mean a lot from now on.

Hiroshi Matsuo:

Thank you, Professor Watai. It is interesting to confirm that the cases can be treated not only by judges but also by other experts in the dispute resolution system as a whole. There may be a possibility to make various ingenuity concerning this topic. Thank you, Ms. Van and Professor Watai.

Today, we are talking about university's contributions to promoting the rule of law. One of the views of the university's contribution is deepening the study of the meaning of the rule of law and how to implement it and proposing legal reforms in the field where necessary rules are missing. I want to also talk about the possibility of collaboration between the teachers to improve the study of law from the viewpoint of comparative law.

From this viewpoint, can I ask Professor Kudo about the possibilities and advantages and problems in collaborative study? Professor Kudo has conducted these kinds of activities by visiting Hanoi Law University and arranging and organizing joint seminars with teachers in partner universities. Professor Kudo, could I ask you some comments from your experience?

Toshitaka Kudo:

Hi. Good afternoon, Professor Matsuo and everybody. I'm Toshitaka Kudo, Associate Professor at Keio University Law School. My major is civil procedure. Last year, I had some opportunities to attend the international workshop and international program at Hanoi Law University. First of all, just in my opinion, the comparative law study is a good opportunity for everybody to think about their own legal system in the global perspective, not only for students but also for scholars.

Last year, I listened to the students' presentations at Hanoi Law University summer program, and I was really impressed because all students did really good jobs. Their presentations were very clear, not to mention that their English were pretty good, maybe better than me. So in my opinion, we professors should provide more opportunities not only for attendees in special programs but also for ordinary students. Still there are some concerns. Because of the COVID-19, we can't give in-person opportunities; we have to do the programs online. It might look easier, but we have challenges, like time zone differences or semester differerences in each country. For example, if it's an end of the semester; it's not a good timing for us to do special programs.

So, why don't we make use of cloud computing or online stuff? Instead of real time presentations, they can just post on YouTube. After receiving comments from viewers in other countries, we can give some feedbacks. We can overcome the time differences by such technologies. Another thing; we have to choose a hot topic. I mean, there is a common issue, but we have a different approach. Such topics would invoke a lot of interest from students.

Now, we are under the challenge of the COVID-19, and definitely would like to beat them. So how should we do? Well, we must wear a mask. But there are a lot of ways to enforce it. Many countries impose fine for not wearing a mask. In some countries, the violators would be jailed. But in Japan, we won't be fined or imprisoned. We wear a mask just as voluntary cooperation. This is an example of a common issue but a different approach. That would make interesting comparative study for us. Why do such differences happen? Because we have different legal backgrounds and people's behaviors. Another point is that we have to choose interesting topics which are discussed globally. That will be a very good opportunity to exchange comparative views not only for students, but also for scholars. That's just my simple idea, but it would be any help hopefully.

Hiroshi Matsuo:

Thank you very much, Professor Kudo. Please continue to extend your international network to do your research on civil procedure and related topics. I very much appreciate Professor Kudo's contribution to the program. We welcome any comments about the collaboration programs or proposals to improve the programs.

Phan Thi Lan Huong:

I think that I would like to add some more from the Hanoi Law University. We have a lot of young lecturers. I think not only student but also teacher exchange is a very good chance for them. If they can come to Keio University by exchange or job exchange program for three months or six months or maybe some visiting professor from Keio can come to Hanoi Law University for short terms, we can do some co-research. We'll do something for publication together. It's the way we can promote our collaboration activity not only for students but also for professors.

Hiroshi Matsuo:

Thank you. We need to improve our collaboration to do some exchanging visiting scholar programs, and we can provide the lectures on web like those conducted owing to the COVID-19 epidemic.

Latdavanh Donkeodavong:

Professor Matsuo, can I add more information about Professor Huong from Hanoi Law University? She is my senior at Nagoya University, and I read the doctoral thesis of Professor Huong about the local reform in Vietnam and platform from Japan. I agree with you that we should have research fellowships or research stays in Laos in Keio University. Like right now, in many countries around the world, they have research stays in law school in many countries like Harvard Law School or whatever. Even in Nagoya University, they have their researchers stay for two months, three months. If Keio University had this program, it would be good. We can share some opinions. We can do joint research between two universities, and we can do a comparative study like the Vietnamese law, Japanese law, Laos law, and Myanmar Law, Cambodian Law. And we can share some ideas on what are the problems, what the issues are, and after that, we can publish the law journal probably by the Keio Law School. It would be good. We can publish a book, a law paper, a law journal. It would be good, and in the future, some time should be spent on this. I just want to add more information about this. Yeah, that's a good idea. Thank you.

Hiroshi Matsuo:

Thank you, Dr. Latdavanh. Proposals are very constructive and productive. As a result of these kinds of collaboration programs, we can also provide the English materials that are used in the lectures to students; this also improves the knowledge sharing among students and teachers in different countries. As I have mentioned, if we use the similar legal terms, for example, some requirements of law such as responsibility in the field of non-performance of contract, but the meaning can be different. So in detail, careful analysis is necessary to deepen understanding of the meaning of the law and legal concepts in each country.

Hitomi Fukasawa:

I got a comment from Mr. Hattapong Hirunrut. Could you introduce him?

Hiroshi Matsuo:

Mr. Hattapong is one of the participants in the programs, and his concerns relate to this symposium. What I want to discuss in today's meeting is how to utilize your knowledge after experiencing the programs. Lawyers must not just study the law but also be involved in practices to bridge the legal system and civil societies. They must disseminate the concept of law and explain to the ordinary people its meaning, the aims, the understanding of the legal concepts, and the legal theory. So I want to ask Mr. Hattapong, who have positively participated in the programs, and he also engages in some practices and practical activities in Thailand. Mr. Hattapong, you have some comments to improve our joint programs to deepen our knowledge of law.

Hattapong Hirunt:

First, I am really happy to come to see you again. First, I want to give a comment on the morning session. I think Power Points materials, which were used in the morning session, should be distributed before the program to students for reading in advance. We students could ask questions and answer each other and participate to find solution or some aspects we don't see. I thought that would have made this seminar more proper than this.

Secondly, I want to recommend that we hold this kind of event every one or two months because now we don't have to go to foreign countries but we can put it in online seminars. We don't need to wait for irregular international conferences.

Universities can hold not only intensive programs such as for seven days or five days, but they can do a program month to month. Like this, we can change pessimistic to optimistic opportunities. We can ask each student in the country to do research on, like, COVID policy in Thailand, Japan, Laos, and we can do comparative study. This can be a really, really good solution for the next academy. I have only two recommendations, sorry, because I was working and listening together, so I don't prepare it properly.

Hiroshi Matsuo:

Thank you very much, Mr. Hattapong. We should implement the request by the first comment immediately for the convenience of participants. The second one will create a new framework for regular joint programs, giving the participants appropriate credit points. I have thought that we would be able to use our trial programs for that purpose. Thank you again for the useful comments.

Hitomi Fukasawa:

Due to unstable internet connection, some participants may have lost discussion points. I wrote three discussion points in the chat box. First is translation of materials. Second is a research collaboration. Third is how we can connect university education with law practice. We have already started discussion on these points, but please feel free to give some comments.

Hiroshi Matsuo:

Thank you. Professor Watai also mentioned the connection between university education and law practice. She introduced the LL.M. program in global legal practice. As she mentioned, the globally practiced standard course includes not just the theoretical program but also some practical programs including the externship programs, which we can design in collaboration with law offices, NGOs, and government ministries.

Hitomi Fukasawa:

Also Mr. Hattapong raised some comments about a study collaboration. In the chat box, Lawyer Takahashi, alumni of Keio LL.M. course, commented that Keio Law School has an intensive study course in every summer vacation or every spring vacation. Yes, but it holds very limited opportunities. Thanks to the internet environment, we can cross over classrooms by using a web meeting system such as Zoom or WebEx. This can help as collaboration study or collaboration learning toward our next step for our program and the promotion of the rule of law.

Hiroshi Matsuo:

Thank you very much. I'd like to ask Mr. Sugita, an active Japanese lawyer, for some comments about the rule of law promotion through the mutual exchange of foreign human resources. In order to improve cooperative activities, it is necessary for us to have more relaxed rules to exchange foreign human resources. But as we know, they have been strict even for

students to go and to come for the study purpose. Mr. Sugita is one of the famous lawyers in this field.

Shohei Sugita:

I'm Shohei Sugita, a practice attorney in Japan and also academic researcher at Keio University Law School. My practice area is immigration law and labor the migration. Last year, the Japanese government decided to make a big policy change to open the labor market to the world. The Japanese government created a new status of residents called the specific skilled worker visa, SSW. International workers with SSW visas can work 14 industrial fields like agriculture, fishery, manufacturing, and so on in Japan. Japan has welcomed highly skilled workers. Japan is having problems with declining birth rate, aging population, and labor shortage; now, 1,660,000 international workers are working in Japan. The number is expected to increase after COVID-19.

What is the role of universities in international labor migration? What is an important role of university education? Usually, educational records are needed to get visa, and the university can provide education in various levels. Universities can also provide research on migration systems. Unfortunately, transparency of labor migration process is very low. There are many problems, such as human rights violations, too much fees, and many brokers. Universities can conduct research to increase transparency of procedures. I think labor migration is a big issue and also a practical and theoretical issue. In Japan and among Asian countries, also we can do well if we cooperate together in this field. I think this is a very good topic for comparative research. Thank you.

Hiroshi Matsuo:

Thank you very much, Mr. Sugita. In order to facilitate the exchange of human resources, the persons who are engaged in law should work to improve the working environment for labor migrants as much as they can. It is a very crucial topic, and Mr. Sugita recommended labor migration issues as a research topic for students. He can be a very good advisor for this research. Mr. Kimpav do you have any comments? He is also a very enthu-siastic participant, and he is a good advisor for students who take part in the PAGLEP in Cambodia.

Mao Kimpav:

Yes, Professor Matsuo. Hello. Thank you for bringing all together here. From my experience during the exchange program, I think that it was a great opportunity. We can learn together from different backgrounds. Some students have already practiced as lawyers, and they are more familiar with practice. However, in different countries, the legal system may be different. Therefore, it would be better if we can have opportunities for students to observe different legal system such as hearing a court case or arbitration. Students can observe what the procedure looks like and how each person participates in it. After students graduate from the program and return their home country, they may have more ideas and compare what are different procedures and what the practices looks like in the court proceeding or in administration.

Hiroshi Matsuo:

Thank you very much, Mr. Kimpav.

Some Japanese students are very grateful to you for your kind support for their research in Cambodia about the Cambodian law and practice. Thank you very much again.

Hitomi Fukasawa:

Mr. Hattapong clarified his comments in chat box.

Hiroshi Matsuo:

Okay. He indicates that we can learn from the COVID epidemic that there are some possibilities to create a new style of collaboration programs. I'd like to continue to improve our cooperative activities to deepen our knowledge of law and understanding of the rule of law promotion. As I indicated in the morning session, it is a long way to go, but we need to be engaged in this kind of activity to improve the situation step by step.

In the presentation session, various perspectives were provided by the presenters. They confirmed different patterns of improvements in the rule of law and what are crucial topics of their concern. But we can learn from our unique experiences.

Today, we have talked about the university's role in improving the rule of law and its possible cooperation with law offices, NGOs, and government ministries. In this context, we cannot overlook the collaboration with the expertized organization for international cooperation. Today, we have a participant from Japan International Cooperation Agency (JICA). Can I ask Mr. Kobayashi from JICA for some comments on the possible collaboration with universities and JICA in the field of legal education?

Yosuke Kobayashi:

Thank you very much for this opportunity. First of all, I was very impressed with all the presentations that were given today, and I learned a lot from all the presentations. In the JICA, with the help of distinguished professors, we have been carrying out legal and judicial development projects in many of the countries the presenters and the participants today represent. At the same time, we through our scholarship program have invited many foreign students to Japan for legal education. It is our observation that our legal and judicial technical assistance and legal scholarships for legal education are similar but in some ways they are separate. We were conducting them separately, but we are now trying to link our technical assistance in the field of legal and judicial development and a scholarship for legal education. So that we can generate more synergy between what we are doing, what we are helping on the ground in developing countries and legal education of these countries.

One example is with the help of Keio University Law School, we are trying to invite people who are closely related to our legal technical assistance to Japan for legal education in Japan, and we would like to create more examples where our legal assistance on the ground and legal education are more closely linked with each other. In that sense, I was very impressed with the comment from Mr. Tharin from Cambodia, who mentioned the need for more disclosure of court judgments in Cambodia. Actually, we are working on that issue through our technical cooperation project in Cambodia, but I did not understand the link or the impact that promoting the

disclosure of court judgments might have on the legal education system in Cambodia. Through a specific example, I learned and think that I was able to understand more deeply about the role of a legal education in promoting the rule of law. Thank you for this opportunity to give my comment.

Hioshi Matsuo:

Thank you very much, Mr. Kobayashi, for your comments on the prospects for our project. The synergy between technical assistance in the judicial and legal field and legal education in the university will open up a new dimension of our challenge for the rule of law promotion. We can foster human resources who will contribute to the legal reform through the collaborated legal education. It will include jurisprudence, comparative law, legal history, law and development, and subjects of the specialized field of law such as civil and civil procedure law, criminal and criminal procedure law, international trade law, international human rights law, environmental law, intellectual property law, international arbitration law, etc. The partner universities can provide them based on their own experiences and valuable teaching materials. As for the legal assistance for the publication of court judgment, which Mr. Kobayashi mentioned, the precedents will become the standard education material. The study of court decisions with making comments on them will improve court judgment and case law formation. I believe it will be an indispensable part of the rule of law promotion.

Before closing the discussion session, let me express my sincere thanks to all participants for sharing many useful insights to promote the rule of law based on our own experiences. I have reconfirmed that we cannot discuss the rule of law as an abstract, uniform, and static ideal from an observer's standpoint. Instead, we should understand it under each country's unique conditions, in its dynamic development process, and through the participation to any part of that process. Starting from our homelands in the Asian region, we can collaborate with other countries to expand the space in which the good laws rule as possible as we can. It will be our contribution to the world in which the rule of law is ubiquitous: it means that anyone, anytime, and anywhere can enjoy the protection of their rights, which we call the rule-of-law-ubiquitous world.

ON-SITE REPORT

FROM LAW CLASSROOMS IN ASIAN UNIVERSITIES:

A Short Report on the Collaboration Program
with Myanmar and the Future Development
of the Common Topic Method

Hitomi Fukasawa*

(Keio University Law School)

1. Introduction

From February 5-13, 2020, Keio University Law School (KLS), located in Tokyo, Japan, in collaboration with the University of Yangon, held the joint program, "Special Study Program on Comparative Customary Law in Japan and Myanmar." Fifteen students participated in the program: five from Japan, eight from Myanmar, and two from Bangladesh.

The program consisted of: (a) lectures on customary laws and their application in Japan and Myanmar; (b)interviews at practical law institutions, such as local courts and law firms; (c) field studies for researching customary rules at local places, such as temples; and (d) presentations and discussions on the Common Topic.

This report introduces the program's activity based on the author's observation. It aims to develop legal education and comparative law discussions in Asian universities by reviewing student presentations and discussions on the Common Topic.

---

* Ph.D. candidate of Keio University Graduate School of Law and Researcher of Law at Keio Institute for Global Law and Development (KEIGLAD).

2. Common Topic Method

2.1 Definition

The Common Topic Method is an original education technique for the study of comparative law in a multinational classroom setting. KLS has used this method in its intensive law program since 2016[1].

The method aims to stimulate comparative law discussions with students from countries with different legal systems. In a multinational law classroom, students come from a civil law system, from the common law tradition, and from countries where the legal system reform is just beginning to develop, such as in Myanmar and Bangladesh. In such a situation, to stimulate comparative law discussions from diverse perspectives, it is necessary to have a core concept to structure talks on the law. The Common Topic can be the core concept for the discussion. The method uses the same fact or case and asks the same set of questions, called the "Common Topic", regardless of students, nationalities.

The same legal topic is expected to clarify differences in law in the approach and the conclusions to problem-solving and in thinking about the application of the law.

Students prepare how the case is solved by applying their home country laws before the class starts. In class, they present their solutions and discuss similarities and differences in problem-solving.

Throughout the preparation, presentation, and discussion cycle, the Common Topic Method enables students to recognize their home country's legal system's characteristics in a relevant, comparative manner.

2.2 Common Topic and Questions

The following law case was presented as a common topic for the assigned students who joined the Myanmar special study program[2].

---

[1] For past program reports, refer Hitomi Fukasawa "From the Law Class Room in Asian Universities Short Report on the Collaboration Program in Vietnam", in: KEIGLAD (ed.), *How Constitutional Law Is Taught in Asian Universities*, Keio University Press, 2020, pp.151-163.

[2] Keio Institute for Global Law and Development (KEIGLAD) opens the common topic to

Mr. A owned certain properties, including pieces of land. A had lived with his wife B and her son C, whose father was Mr. D, who had died before Ms. B married Mr. A. Mr. A had two children, daughter E and son F, whose mother was G. Mr. A, and Ms. G were divorced.

Mr. A had made a last will and testament that stipulated that all inheritance shall be given to Ms. E. after Mr. A dies. However, before Ms. E registered the acquisition of A's heritage, Mr. F applied for the registration of the acquisition of a share of one-fourth of the piece of land, which was included in A's inheritance, following the provision of legal inheritance. He then sold the share to Mr. H, who registered it. Mr. H knew that Mr. A had stipulated in his testamentary that all his inheritance shall be given to Ms. E.

Question 1

Who are the heirs of Mr. A in your legal system, and how is the share of each heir determined?

Can Mr. C be the heir of Mr. A and receive A's inheritance? If so, how much of Mr. C's inheritance can Mr. C receive?

Question 2

Can the heirs sell their shares of each property, such as a piece of land included in the inheritance, to a third party, even before the division of the inheritance?

Question 3

Can Ms. E claim the invalidity of the transaction of the share of the piece of land between F and H to annul the registration?

This Common Topic is a simple inheritance law case. It tries to clarify differences between the inheritance systems of Myanmar, Bangladesh, and Japan

the public. As for details, please access KEIGLAD, http://keiglad.keio.ac.jp/wp/wp-content/uploads/2020/06/Myanmar_externship_presentation_Myanmar_2020.pdf (Last accessed on 30 November 2020).

Figure: The Common Topic Case

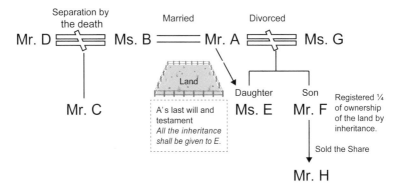

through three questions.

Question 1 is about who can be an heir in law in each country's inheritance law. Mainly, it asks whether a stepchild, Mr. C, can inherit from a stepfather, Mr. A, or not.

Question 2 asks about whether an heir can transfer inherited assets before the estate is split. The purpose of the question is to analyze whether assets belong to heirs before the division of the inheritance.

Questions 3 asks about the validity of a will. Students must analyze a statutory inheritance and the effect of a will in each country. If a will is valid, an heir, Ms. E, could inherit the entire piece of land. However, a share of the land was transacted from an heir, Mr. F, to a third party, Mr. H. It is necessary to consider the security of the transaction for a third party. Furthermore, if a third party knows about the will, which legal discussion point should be prioritized, the will or the transaction?

How did the participants analyze the case and answer each question? Section 3 provides the students' presentations.

3. Student Presentations

3.1 Myanmar

Myanmar has no legislation for inheritance. Instead of statute law legislated by the parliament, customary laws apply to inheritance cases. The customary law that applies to inheritance cases depends on the religion to which the parties adhere. For example, Buddhist customary law applies to adherents of Buddhism, Islamic law applies to Muslim parties, and Hindu law applies to Hindu parties. Myanmar students answered the case questions based on Buddhist customary law, which is the majority religion for Myanmarese.

Upon a person's death, Buddhist customary law decides the order of the deceased's heirs in the following order: (1) spouse; (2) descendants; (3) brothers and sisters; (4) parents; and (5) uncles and aunts.

According to this law, as to Question 1, Mr. A's wife B, daughter E, and son F can succeed Mr. A. C can also succeed his stepfather because Buddhist customary law does not distinguish between biological children and stepchildren.

Students also explained how the portion of the estate that each heir receives is decided under Buddhist law. According to two Myanmarese Supreme Court precedents (Maung Ba Wai Vs. Mi Sar U, 2L.B.R, 174FB, and Ma E Nyunt Vs. Daw Ma Get, AIR, 1938 Ran 293), the court judged that children inherit three-quarters of the inheritance and a spouse inherits one-quarter. Therefore, wife B inherits a quarter of A's property, and children C, E, and F inherit three-quarters of his estate.

Regarding Question 2, students analyzed that the validity of the transaction may be an issue. Unlike inheritance, the Transfer of Property Act 1882 provides general rules for a share in Myanmar[3]. Section 6 of the Act stipulates that "property of any kind may be transferred, except as otherwise provided by this Act or by any other law for the time being in force." Paragraph (a) provides that "the chance of an heir-apparent succeeding to an estate, the chance of a relation obtaining a legacy on the death of a kinsman, or any other mere possibility of a

---

[3] *The Transfer of Property Act* (1882), https://www.mlis.gov.mm/lsScPop.do?lawordSn=8490 (last accessed on January 5th 2020).

like nature, cannot be transferred." The Myanmarese Supreme Court also judged that the person who has the potential to inherit could not sell or transfer by other means their shares of the inheritance before the division of inheritance took place, under Section 6 (a) of the Transfer of Property Act (W. Dhar Vs. Htoon May and others, 12, BLT,106). Students concluded that the transfer of shares before the inheritance division is invalid under the Myanmarese legal system. In this sense, as to Question 3, E can claim the invalidity of the transaction between F and H because it is illegal according to the Transfer of Property Act 1882 Section 6 (a).

However, students concluded that E could not inherit the entire piece of land since Buddhist law does not recognize wills. Therefore, heirs inherit the land according to the general provisions of succession rule under Buddhist law.

3.2 Bangladesh

Like Myanmar, Bangladesh also applies customary law to inheritance cases, and applicable customary law is also decided by which religion the parties follow. Bangladeshi students presented their answers based on Islamic law, as the majority of Bangladeshi are Muslim.

The Quran and the Hadith are the sources of inheritance rule for Muslims. The Quran Chapter 4 Section 11 (4:11) describes inheritance rules for children[4], and Section 12 (4:12) is about inheritance rules for wives[5]. As to heirs, the stu-

---

[4] "An-Nisa [The Women]", *Quran*, 4:11, Allah commands you regarding your children: the share of the male will be twice that of the female. If you leave only two or more females, their share is two-thirds of the estate. But if there is only one female, her share will be one-half. Each parent is entitled to one-sixth if you leave offspring. But if you are childless and your parents are the only heirs, then your mother will receive one-third. But if you leave siblings, then your mother will receive one-sixth—after the fulfilment of bequests and debts. Be fair to your parents and children, as you do not ′fully know who is more beneficial to you. This is an obligation from Allah. Surely Allah is All-Knowing, All-Wise.

[5] *Ibid.* 4:12, You will inherit half of what your wives leave if they are childless. But if they have children, then your share is one-fourth of the estate—after the fulfilment of bequests and debts. And your wives will inherit one-fourth of what you leave if you are childless. But if you have children, then your wives will receive one-eighth of your estate—after the ful-

dents explained that A's wife Ms. B, his daughter Ms. E and his son Mr. F, are heirs of Mr. A. However, Mr. C, the stepchild, cannot succeed Mr. A because the word "children," which appeared in 4:11, is interpreted as "biological children" in Bangladesh. In contrast with Myanmar, a stepchild is not considered an heir of stepparents.

A wife can succeed a one-eighth portion of the assets (4:12), and children receive the remaining share. However, the portion for children varies based on sex. Chapter 4 Section 11 describes that "the share of the male will be twice that of the female." Therefore, in answer to Question 1, the students concluded that the portion of Mr. F's son is seven-twelfths, while Ms. E, a daughter, receives as her portion the equivalent of 7/24 of Mr. A's assets.

As to Question 2, the students explained that heirs could sell their shares before the inheritance division without mentioning any specific Islamic law. Although if they sell more than their legal portion, they must return the excess property. Therefore, Mr. F must return the part which exceeds his legal portion.

Regarding the validity of a will, which is the main point of discussion in Question 3, Islamic law allows wills. However, the Hadith provides that a will cannot exceed one-third of the deceased's property[6]. The students concluded that Ms. E could not claim the invalidity of the transaction between Mr. F and Mr. H. Ms. E cannot succeed the entire piece of land as long as Islamic law does not allow any wills that may exceed one-third of the deceased's property.

3.3 Japan

In contrast with Myanmar and Bangladesh, the Japanese Civil Code (JCC) applies to Japan's inheritance cases. It is a law enacted by the Diet but is influ-

---

filment of bequests and debts. And if a man or a woman leaves neither parents nor children but only a brother or a sister from their mother's side`, they will each inherit one-sixth, but if they are more than one, they all will share one-third of the estate—after the fulfilment of bequests and debts without harm to the heirs. This is a commandment from Allah. And Allah is All-Knowing, Most Forbearing.

[6] Muhammad al-Bukhari "80 Law of Inheritance", 725, *Sahih al-Bukhari,* Volume 8, https://muflihun.com/bukhari/80/725 (last accessed on 3rd January 2021).

enced by the modern legal system in Western countries rather than Japanese traditions and customs.

As to Question 1, JCC article 887 to 890 stipulates legal heirs. A spouse is a legal heir of the dead spouse (JCC 890), and a child is also a legal heir of his or her parents (JCC 887).

Regarding the stepchild's legal status, Japanese students concluded that a stepchild could not be a legal heir to his stepparents unless he or she is legally adopted. Therefore, wife B, daughter E, and son F are legal heirs in Japan. This conclusion was the same in Bangladesh.

However, each heir's statutory share was different. In Japan, JCC article 900 establishes a portion of statutory share, and its article paragraph (i) is about the case in which a child and a spouse are heirs. In such a situation, a child and a spouse shall each inherit one half. Thus, wife B inherits one-half, and his children, Ms. E and Mr. F, inherit one-fourth each from Mr. A's assets. There is no difference in treatment between a son and a daughter. A wife receives a greater portion in Japan than in Bangladesh.

As to Question 2, the JCC posits that if there are two or more heirs, the inherited property shall be co-owned by the heirs until the division of inherited property takes place (898). The general rule for the co-owned property shall be applied for co-owned inheritance cases (JCC 249). It is necessary to get approval from the other co-owners if one co-owner wants to sell the entire co-owned property (JCC 251). However, the JCC allows each co-owner to sell their share without the other co-owners' approval because it is considered private property. Based on the analysis of Question 1, Mr. F has a one-fourth share of the inherited property. Therefore, he can sell his share to Mr. H by himself.

Regarding Question 3, the JCC allows writing a will. The will that stipulates Ms. E shall inherit the entirety of A's land after his death is valid. Upon A's death, only E can be the owner of the land. In this sense, the transaction between Mr. H and Mr. F may be invalid because Mr. F bought a share from Mr. H, who does not have any shares of the land.

However, the law should consider protections for a third party who reasonably believes that an heir would have the right to dispose of their share. It may sometimes be the case that heirs do not recognize the existence of the will itself.

Moreover, as explained above, the JCC allows an heir to freely dispose of their share of the inherited property before the inheritance division. At the same time, there is the problem that a third party has no way of knowing the contents of the will. Solving this issue, JCC article 899-2, which was promogulated in 2020, provides that if an heir's inheritance exceeds the statutory portion, they cannot claim their property right to a third party without registration. According to this new provision, E cannot claim her right to the land, exceeding the one-fourth sold to Mr. H, without land registration.

Though, in this case, H knew that E would inherit the entire piece of land according to the terms of the will. There is a question that an heir could claim ownership without land registration to a third party who knows that an heir inherited more than the statutory portion. There has not been a concrete answer to this question yet, as it is a new article. Japanese students tried to answer this question by referring to a similar law discussion on JCC article 177, which is a case about the double sale of land and land registration.

JCC article 177 provides that acquisitions of, losses of, and real rights changes to immovable properties may not be asserted against third parties unless registration takes place. This article's interpretation is an issue in the case of a double land transaction. In such a case, the owners cannot assert their ownership to others. The law tries to decide the order by the timing of land registration. Thus, they cannot claim their land ownership to others without land registration, and a person who registers first can assert their ownership. However, sometimes it causes a legal conflict, especially if a second buyer knows that the first buyer has not yet registered the land. The second buyer registered it before the first buyer.

Some Japanese legal scholars claim that the first buyer can assert their land ownership to the second buyer without a land registration because the second buyer knows that the first buyer has not yet registered. However, the Japanese Supreme Court judged that a first buyer might assert his land ownership without a land registration if a second buyer knows the first buyer has not registered, plus he has an intention to damage the first buyer's property right.

Referring to this judgment, Japanese students answered that Ms. E could not assert her ownership of the land that exceeds the statutory portion without the land registration. Mr. H knew about the will's content, but he did not have the intention to harm Ms. E's property right. They, therefore, concluded that Ms. E could not claim that the contract between Mr. F and Mr. H was invalid.

The chart describes a summary of students' presentations. What students discussed at the class? The next Section provides the students' discussion.

Chart: Summary of Students' Presentations

	Myanmar	Bangladesh	Japan
Question 1	Mr A'Heirs (Portion)		
Wife B	○ (1/4)	○ (3/24)	○ (1/2)
Stepchild C	○ (1/4)	×	×
Daughter E	○ (1/4)	○ (7/24)	○ (1/4)
Son F	○ (1/4)	○ (14/24)	○ (1/4)
Question 2	Share Transfer before the Division of the Inheritance		
Answer	× Shall not be allowed by Buddhism Law	○ Shall not be allowed transaction exceeds the portion	○
Question 3	Writing a Will		
Answer	× Shall not be allowed by Buddhism Law	○ Shall not be allowed a will exceeds 1/3 of assets	○

4. Discussion Session

A Japanese civil law professor moderated the discussion. The another professor of private international law was also joined.

The moderator picked the stepchild's right of inheritance as a first discussion point. To stimulate the discussion, he introduced a historical fact that the former

JCC recognized a stepchild's right to inheritance. In the past, a household was a traditional Japanese family structure, under which a stepchild is also a member of the household. This traditional family system prioritized household harmony over the individual rights of each member. A head of household managed all properties and took care of all household members. However, household members could not oppose his decisions. As time passed, this system was considered outdated, which was viewed as sacrificing family members' rights for the good of keeping harmony in the family. The JCC eliminated the traditional concept of the household in the process of the Japanese legal reform that took place after World War II, which respected the dignity of individual rights. Inheritance rights for stepchildren disappeared because the household on which the right was based also disappeared.

On this point, a Myanmarese student questioned if any Japanese opposed the change to the law or not that stepchildren could not inherit from stepparents after the amendment. Japanese students supposed that most Japanese supported the legal amendment because they also thought the household system was an antiquated tradition.

The moderator asked if, in the case that a stepchild does not have statutory inheritance rights, if a will is an option to inherit stepparents' assets. In Bangladesh, a stepchild may inherit one-third from the stepparents if there is a will. On this point, a Japanese student asked why a person cannot leave a will that exceeds one-third of the estate in Bangladesh. Bangladeshi students answered that they also did not know why, but that there is no room for changing Islamic law.

In contrast to Bangladesh and Japan, Myanmar's Buddhist law does not recognize a will. Some students asked what a person in Myanmar can do if he wants to leave his property to a specific person. Myanmarese students commented that gifts or family arrangements could be an option in such a case. Both systems allow leaving specific property to a specific person and carrying out the transfer before death. The gift is an agreement between two parties, grantor and grantee, while the family arrangement only requires participation from family members, a lawyer, and two witnesses.

Students' Discussion at the Class (Yangon, Myanmar, 12 February 2020)

A Myanmarese student considered that a family arrangement is better than a will. While a will is a unilateral legal act, all family members can join the family arrangement and discuss inheritance, which they will face in the future. Participation in family arrangements reduces legal conflicts regarding inheritance cases.

The discussion started from small differences that appeared among the answers to each question, and gradually developed into the essential and primary questions on the legal substance in each country.

Some students commented about the possibility of amending Islamic law. They seemed to feel that the Islamic law inheritance rule is unfair to women. Bangladeshi students were of the strong opinion that religious law should apply to family and inheritance matters in Bangladesh. Muslims must follow the Quran, and this cannot be changed. For a while, they tried to find a solution through discussion, but none was found. The professor of private international law suggested that changing customary law is very challenging. However, citizens can decide which law should be applied for inheritance by political decision-making. The parliament could change the legislation such that statutory law applied to matters of inheritance instead of customary law.

Myanmarese students asked Japanese students how the Japanese felt about the current inheritance law system. To clarify their point, they explained the history of inheritance law in Myanmar. When Burma was colonized by the British, the British Council did not allow Buddhists to leave wills because writing a will was a legal act reserved for Christians. Based on their experience, Japanese inheritance rules seemed similar to Christian rules, in that they wondered if the legal rules conformed to Japanese society or not. However, Japanese students were at a loss as to how to reply.

Legal pluralism was also a topic of discussion. The Japanese students commented that multiple customary laws might sometimes cause inconveniences. For example, which customary law should be applied if each family member believes in a different religion?

At the end of the discussion, the private international law professor commented that the choice of law is the primary issue in private international law. In this sense, it is necessary to know about the legal contexts in other countries. In Myanmar, Bangladesh, and Japan, heirs automatically receive an inheritance. However, a settlement is necessary to inherit property in the UK or the U.S. This, it is necessary to consider not only religion but also national contexts for international inheritance cases.

5. Summary and Findings

Throughout the presentation and discussion, participants were able to understand how the Common Topic legal case was solved in a different country. They learned that customary law is a primary legal basis of inheritance in Myanmar and Bangladesh, while JCC legislation is the essential law for inheritance in Japan. Even in a country where customary law is applied, Buddhist law and Islamic law reached different outcomes.

The students were also able to analyze the case from the standpoint of practical law because private international law became one of the discussion points. It is possible that practical lawyers must interpret a specific customary law for an international inheritance case as a result of the choice of law, even though his or her country does not recognize the customary law. In this sense, the presentations went beyond the mere introduction of foreign laws.

In the discussion, many questions were asked about why a country has a particular legal system, for example in the case of why a will cannot exceed one-third of assets under Islamic law. To answer such kinds of questions, looking back on history is essential. Perhaps there are historical reasons, as in the case of the British Council not allowing Myanmar Buddhists to write wills.

From a historical and legal perspective, participants also asked essential points about the Japanese system of inheritance law. There was the incident where Japanese students couldn't reply to Myanmarese students when they were asked about Japanese awareness of the current inheritance law. It was not a language issue that made it difficult to explain in English, but rather perhaps because the JCC eliminated the customs and traditions that existed in Japanese society in the past. Law school students, who focus on the interpretation of legal study, do not have the opportunity to think about legal development in Japan. Such fundamental questions about a legal system give law students opportunities to be aware of the importance of the relationship between law, society, culture, and history.

At the end of the discussion, a difficult but essential question was raised: how customary law can change when its contents represent a gap with society. One solution pointed out was to adopt legislation through the parliament. However, to enact a law through parliament in a democratic manner requires the full participation of the nation. Because customary law is rooted in society, some people support it. The discussion showed the path of changing a customary law through legislation, but the difficulty of this path was also made clear.

Overall, the program can have fruitful presentations and discussions. Some discussion topics, such as those related to history, should be continuously researched and the results shared with participants. The program was an intensive law program, for which ongoing communication is necessary. Holding a wrap-up class is one solution to share new findings.

6. Conclusion and Further Development for the Common Topic Method

KLS has conducted an intensive law program twice a year since 2016 using the Common Topic Method. The method is a useful law education tool to stimulate comparative legal discussions in a multinational classroom with students from various countries as analyzed in Section 5.

However, KLS faced a new crisis in 2020. The coronavirus pandemic of 2019 (COVID-19) forced universities to postpone all in-person international programs. For better or worse, the pandemic has accelerated online education programs at universities globally. KLS also held an intensive law program online in September 2020 with partner universities in Southeast Asia.

The September program's main topic was the promotion of the rule of law. It consisted of: (a) contemporary lectures about legal issues related to the rule of law in Vietnam, Thailand, Laos, Myanmar, Cambodia, and Japan[7]; (b)interviews at practical law institutions, including international law firms, the legal assistance project office, and NGOs; (c) cultural exchanges; and (d) presentations about the promotion of the rule of law in the students' countries and discussion.

In the presentation and discussion, the participants evaluated the situation of the rule of law in their home countries and discussed various legal issues related to the rule of law, including legal aid services for children, women, and other underrepresented people; the multi-party system; control of political power; transparency of the government; and the differences in the rule of law.

The online version of the program was comparable to the past five years' intensive law programs in a real classroom. Since the travel expenses could be saved, the online program is accessible for students who were unable to participate for financial reasons. On the other hand, studying abroad offers unique intercultural opportunities, such as communicating with participants after class and having an immersion experience in a different country's culture and environment. This, unfortunately, was lost.

---

[7] Part 1, Chapter 1 to 7 are based on lectures in the September program.

The momentum in the development of international online programs may not stop, even after the pandemic of COVID-19. The Internet can help following-up on the program and with ongoing discussions, for example, on the possibility of customary law changes by legislation discussed in the Myanmar program.

The next subject is the development of law programs and promotion of the Common Topic Method through online programming[8].

---

[8] On the basic idea of the Common Topic Method and its application samples, see Hiroshi Matsuo, "Use of Common Topics to Improve Comparative Law and Legal Education in Asia," in: KEIGLAD (ed.), *How Civil Law Is Taught in Asian Universities* (PAGLEP Series III), Keio University Press, 2019, pp. 243-263; id., "Use of Common Topic Method to Promote Inclusive Legal Education," in: KEIGLAD (ed.), *How Public Law Is Taught in Asian Universities* (PAGLEP Series IV), Keio University Press, 2020, pp. 135-149.

INDEX

ABOUT KEIGLAD

KEIGLAD - Keio Institute for Global Law and Development

Keio Institute for Global Law and Development (KEIGLAD) was established for the purpose of assisting the promotion of international exchange and international cooperation among researchers, students, and staffs for legal study and legal education. KEIGLAD will promote the concerned projects as follow:

- Promotion of the Program for Asian Global Legal Professions (PAGLEP)
- Collection of information on the concerned comparative law
- Collection of information on the method of legal education
- Provision of materials for legal education
- Provision of information and support for foreign students who will study at Keio Law School and Keio Law School students who will study abroad
- Promotion of the concerned symposiums and research meetings
- Publication of working papers
- Other matters concerned with objectives of KEIGLAD

Through these activities, KEIGLAD aims to contribute to the promotion of "Rule-of-Law-Ubiquitous Society", in which Anyone can access to justice Anywhere and Anytime.

ABOUT THE AUTHORS[*]

Isao Kitai
Professor, Dean, Keio University Law School, Japan

Hiroshi Matsuo
Professor, Keio University Law School; Director, Keio Institute for Glabal Law and Development (KEIGLAD), Japan

Ronnakorn Bunmee
Assistant Professor, Faculty of Law, Thammasat University, Thailand

Phan Thi Lan Huong
Deputy Head, International Cooperation Department, Hanoi Law University, Vietnam; Head, Representative Office of Nagoya University in Vietnam

Reginald M. Pastrana
Chief Technical Advisor, Luxembourg Agency for Development Cooperation (LuxDev), Laos

Latdavanh Donkeodavong
Deputy Head of Research and Academic Service Division, Faculty of Law and Political Science, National University of Laos

Khin Phone Myint Kyu
Professor, Department of Law, University of Yangon, Myanmar

Khin Khin Su
Lecturer, Department of Law, University of Yangon, Myanmar

Dao Gia Phuc

Vice-Director of the American Law Center, University of Economics and Law, Vietnam National University in Ho Chi Minh city, Vietnam

Hitomi Fukasawa

Researcher, KEIGLAD, Japan

* For the contributors to Discussion in Part II, see Participants list on page 135.

MEXT/JSPS Re-Inventing Japan Project (Type B: ASEAN) FY 2016
文部科学省　平成 28 年度大学の世界展開力事業（ASEAN 地域における大学間交流の推進）
タイプ B 採択プログラム

Promoting the Rule of Law in Asian Dynamics
Programs for Asian Global Legal Professions Series V

2021 年 2 月 20 日　初版第 1 刷発行

編　者————KEIGLAD
発行者————KEIGLAD
　　　　　　（慶應義塾大学大学院法務研究科グローバル法研究所）
　　　　　　代表者　松尾　弘
　　　　　　〒 108-8345　東京都港区三田 2-15-45
　　　　　　TEL 03-5427-1574
発売所————慶應義塾大学出版会株式会社
　　　　　　〒 108-8346　東京都港区三田 2-19-30
　　　　　　TEL 03-3451-3584　FAX 03-3451-3122
装　丁————鈴木　衛
組　版————株式会社 STELLA
印刷・製本——中央精版印刷株式会社
カバー印刷——株式会社太平印刷社